Theism or Atheism

Chapman Cohen

The present edition is a revised version of this work, produced in the current edition with completely new, easy to read format, and is set and proofread by Alfred Aghajanian for Indo-European Publishing.

IndoEuropean
Publishing.com
Los Angeles CA, USA

Preface

Shrouded in the cloak of philosophy, the question of the existence of God continues to attract attention, and, I may add, to command more respect than it deserves. For it is only by a subterfuge that it assumes the rank of philosophy. "God" enters into philosophy only when it is beginning to lose caste in its proper home, and then in its new environment it undergoes such a transformation as to contain very little likeness to its former, and proper, self. It disowns its parentage and claims another origin, and, like so many genealogists devising pedigrees for the parvenu, certain philosophers attempt to map out for the newcomer an ancestry to which he can establish no valid claim. Nothing would, indeed, surprise the ancestor more than to be brought face to face with his descendant. He would not be more astonished than would the ancient Eohippus on meeting with a modern dray-horse. In anthropology or history the idea of God may fairly claim a place, but it has no place in philosophy on any sensible meaning of the word.

The consequence of this transference of the idea of God to the sphere of philosophy is the curious position that the God in which people believe is not the God whose existence is made the product of an argument, and the God of the argument is not the God of belief. The theory and the fact have no more likeness to each other than a chestnut horse has to a horse-chestnut. A fallacy is perpetuated by appealing to a fact, but the fact immediately discredits the fallacy by disowning it in practice. The grounds upon which the belief in God is supposed to rest, the reasoning from which it springs, are seen to follow the belief instead of preceding it. The roots are in the air, and on closer inspection are seen to be artificial adornments, so many imitations that have been hung there for the purpose of imposing on near-sighted or careless observers.

The purpose of the following pages is to make clear the nature of this alliance and to expose the real character of what we are asked to worship. There are, of course, many on whose ears any amount of reasoning will fall without effect. To that class this book will not appeal; it may be questioned whether many will even read it. They will go on professing the belief they have always professed, and taking pride in the fact that they have an intellect which is superior to proof, and which disdains evidence when it runs contrary to "my belief." Others will, I expect, complain that the treatment of so solemn a subject is not "reverent" enough. But why *any* subject should be treated reverently, as a condition of examination, is more than I have ever been able to discover. It is asking the inquirer to commence his investigation with a half-promise to find something good in what he is about to examine. Whether a thing is worthy of reverence or not is a conclusion that must follow investigation, not precede it. And one does not observe any particular reverence shown by the religious person towards those beliefs in which he does not happen to believe.

But there are some who will read thoughtfully an examination of so old a subject as Theism, and it is to those that these pages are addressed. One cannot hope to say anything that is strikingly new on so well worn a subject as the existence of God, but there are many who will read an old subject when presented in a new work, and even then there is also the possibility of presenting an old topic in a slightly new form. And I think these will find the main lines of the defense set up by the Goddite dealt with in a manner that should at least make the point at issue clear.

Finally, it is one aim of this book to press home the point that the logical issue is between Theism and Atheism. That there is no logical halting place between the two, and that any attempt to call a halt is little more than a concession to a desire for mental or social convenience, seems to me as clear as anything can well be. And there is really nothing gained, ultimately, by the halt. Disinclination on the part of the non-Theist to push the issue to its logical conclusion is treated by the Theist as inability to do so, and is used as an argument in support of his own belief. In matters of the intellect, compromise is almost always a dangerous policy. It heartens one's enemies and disheartens one's friends. And there is really no adequate reason why those who have given up belief in deity should continue to treat this master superstition of the ages as though it were one of our most valuable inheritances, to be surrendered with lowered heads and sinking hearts. We who know both sides know that in giving up the belief in deity we have lost nothing of value, nothing that need cause us a single regret. And on that point we certainly can speak with authority; for we have been where the Theist is, he has not been where we are. Many of us know quite well all that is meant by the fear and trembling with which the believer looks upon a world without God. And we know how idle the fear is—as idle as a child's fear of the dark. What the world is like *with* God, there is all the experience of history to inform us; and it would indeed be strange if love and brotherhood, armed with the weapons that science has given us, could not produce a better human society than has ever existed under the dominion of the Gods.

Contents

Part I

AN EXAMINATION OF THEISM

Chapter I

What is God?

Soon after that famous Atheist, Charles Bradlaugh, entered the House of Commons, it is said that a fellow member approached him with the remark, "Good God, Bradlaugh, what does it matter whether there is a God or not?" Bradlaugh's answer is not recorded, but one is impelled to open the present examination of the belief in God, by putting the same question in another form. Is the belief in God, as we are so often assured, one of the most important questions that can engage the attention of man? Under certain conditions one can conceive a rational answer in the affirmative. Where the mental and social conditions are such that men seriously believe the incidence of natural forces on mankind to be determined by the direct action of "God," one can appreciate right belief concerning him being treated as of first rate importance. In such circumstances wrong ideas are the equivalent of disaster. But we are not in that condition to-day. It is, indeed, common ground with all educated men and women that natural happenings are independent of divine control to at least the extent that natural forces affect all alike, and without the least reference to religious beliefs. Fire burns and water drowns, foods sustain and poisons kill, no matter what our opinions on theology may be. In an earthquake or a war there is no observable relation between casualties and religious opinions. We are, in fact, told by theologians that it is folly to expect that there should be. A particular providence is no longer in fashion; God, we are told, works only through general laws, and that is only another way of saying that our opinions about God have no direct or observable influence on our well-being. It is a tacit admission that human welfare depends upon our knowledge and manipulation of the forces by which we are surrounded. There *may* be a God behind these forces, but that neither determines the extent of our knowledge of them or our power to manipulate them. The belief in God becomes a matter of, at best, secondary importance, and quite probably of no importance whatever.

But if that be so why bother about the belief? Is that not a reason for leaving it alone and turning our attention to other matters? The answer to that is that the belief in God is not of so detached a character as this advice assumes. In the course of ages the belief in God has acquired associations that give it the character of a highly obstructive force. It has become so entangled with inculcated notions of right and wrong that it is everywhere used as a buttress for institutions which have either outgrown their utility, or are in need of serious modification in the interests of the race. The opposition encountered in any attempt to deal with marriage, divorce, or education, are examples of the way in which religious ideas are permitted to interfere with subjects that should be treated solely from the standpoint of social utility. The course of human development has been such that religion has hitherto occupied a commanding position in relation to social laws and customs, with the result that it is often found difficult to improve either until the obstructive influence of religious beliefs has been dealt with.

It is not, then, because I believe the question of the existence of God to be of intrinsic importance that an examination of its validity is here undertaken. Its importance to-day is of a purely

3

contingent character. The valid ground for now discussing its truth is that it is at present allowed to obstruct the practical conduct of life. And under similar circumstances it would be important to investigate the historical accuracy of Old Mother Hubbard or Jack and the Beanstalk. Any belief, no matter what its nature, must be dealt with as a fact of some social importance, so long as it is believed by large numbers to be essential to the right ordering of life. Whether true or false, beliefs are facts—mental and social facts, and the scheme of things which leaves them out of account is making a blunder of the most serious kind.

Certainly, conditions were never before so favorable for the delivery of a considered judgment on the question of the belief in God. On the one side we have from natural science an account of the universe which rules the operations of deity out of court. And on the other side we have a knowledge of the mode of origin of the belief which should leave us in no doubt as to its real value. We hope to show later that the question of origin is really decisive; that in reaching conclusions concerning the origin of the god-idea we are passing judgment as to its value. That the masters of this form of investigation have not usually, and in so many words, pushed their researches to their logical conclusions is no reason why we should refrain from doing so. Facts are in themselves of no great value. It is the conclusions to which they point that are the important things.

If the conclusions to which we refer are sound, then the whole basis of theism crumbles away. If we are to regard the god-idea as an evolution which began in misunderstandings of nature that were rooted in the ignorance of primitive man, it would seem clear that no matter how refined or developed the idea may become, it can rest on no other or sounder basis than that which is presented to us in the psychology of primitive man.

4

Each stage of theistic belief grows out of the preceding stage, and if it can be shown that the beginning of this evolution arose in a huge blunder I quite fail to see how any subsequent development can convert this unmistakable blunder into a demonstrable truth. To take a case in point. When it was shown that so far as witchcraft rested on observed facts these could be explained on grounds other than those of the malevolent activities of certain old women, the belief in witchcraft was not "purified," neither did it advance to any so-called higher stage; it was simply abandoned as a useless and mischievous explanation of facts that could be otherwise accounted for. Are we logically justified in dealing with the belief in God on any other principle? We cannot logically discard the world of the savage and still retain his interpretation of it. If the grounds upon which the savage constructed his theory of the world, and from which grew all the ghosts and gods with which he believed himself to be surrounded, if these grounds are false, how can we still keep in substance to conclusions that are admittedly based on false premises? We can say with tolerable certainty that had primitive man known what we know about nature the gods would never have been born. Civilized man does not discover gods, he discards them. It was a profound remark of Feurbach's, that religion is ultimately anthropology, and it is anthropology that gives to all forms of theism the death blow.

In our own time, at least, it is not difficult to see that the word God retains its influence with many because of the indefinite manner in which it is used. It is never easy to say what a person has in his mind when he uses the word. In most cases one would be safe in saying that nothing at all is meant. It is just one of those "blessed" words where the comfort felt in their use is proportionate to the lack of definite meaning that accompanies them. A frank confession of ignorance is something that most people heartily dislike, and where problems are persistent and difficult of solution what most people are in search of is a narcotic. That "God" is one of the most popular of narcotics will be denied by none who study the psychology of the average man or woman.

When not used as a narcotic, "God" is brought into an argument as though it stood for a term which carried a well defined and well understood meaning. In work after work dealing with theism one looks in vain for some definition of "God." All that one can do is to gather the author's meaning from the course of his argument, and that is not always an easy task. The truth is, of course, that instead of the word carrying with it a generally understood meaning there is no word that is more loosely used or which carries a greater variety of meanings. Its connotations are endless, and range from the aggressively man-like deity of the primitive savage up—or down—to the abstract force of the mathematical physicist and the shadowy "Absolute" of the theologizing metaphysician. The consequence of this is to find commonly that while it is one kind of a god that is being set up in argument, it is really another god that is being defended and even believed in. When we find people talking of entering into communion with God, or praying to God, it is quite certain they do not conceive him as a mere mathematical abstraction, or as a mere symbol of an unknown force. It is impossible to conceive any sane man or woman extracting comfort from praying or talking to a god who could not think, or feel, or hear. And if he possesses qualities that the religious attitude implies, we endow him with all the attributes of personality, and, be it noted, of human personality. Either one God is believed in – in fact while another is established in theory – or an elaborate argument is presented which serves no other purpose than a disguise for the fact that there is no genuine belief left.

An example of the misleading way in which words are used is

supplied by Sir Oliver Lodge, who for a man of science shows an amazing capacity for making use of unscientific language. In his "Man and the Universe," discussing the attributes of deity, he says, "Let no worthy attribute be denied to the deity. In anthropomorphism there are many errors, but there is one truth. Whatever worthy attributes belong to man, be it personality or any other, its existence in the universe is thereby admitted; it belongs to the all." Putting on one side the fallacy involved in speaking of attributes as though they were good or bad in themselves, one wonders why Sir Oliver limits this inference to the "worthy" attributes? Unworthy attributes are as real as worthy ones. If honesty exists so does dishonesty. Kindness is as real as cruelty. And if we must credit the deity with possessing all the good attributes, to whom must we credit the bad ones? A little later Sir Oliver does admit that we must credit the deity with the bad attributes also, but adds that they are dying out. But as they are *part* of the deity, their decay must mean that the deity is also undergoing a process of change, of education, and is as much subject to the law of growth as we are. Surely that is not what people mean when they speak about God. A god who is only a part of the cosmic process ceases to be a god in any reasonable sense of the term.

Professor Mellone, in his "God and the World," says that the word God "becomes a name for the infinite system of law regarded as a whole" (p. 122). If that were really all that was meant by the word the matter would not be worth discussing. "God" as a symbol of a generalization is a mere name, and as such is as good as any other name. But, again, it is plain that people mean more than that when they speak about God. If God is a name for universal law, let any really religious man try the plan of substituting in his prayers and in his thoughts the phrase "Universal Law" for "God," and then see how long he will retain his religion. As Mr. Balfour points out ("Theism and Humanism," p. 20), the god of religion and the god of philosophy represent two distinct beings, and it is hard to see how the two can be fused into one. The plain truth is that it is impossible to now make the existence of the god of religion reasonable, and the plan adopted is that of arguing for the existence of something about which there is often no dispute, and then introducing as the product of the argument something that has never been argued for at all. It is the philosophic analogue of the hat and omelet trick.

In this connection some well considered words of Sir James Frazer are well worth noting. He says:—

By a god I understand a superhuman and supernatural being, of a spiritual and personal nature, who controls the world or some part of it on the whole for good, and who is endowed with intellectual faculties, moral feelings, and active powers, which we can only conceive on the analogy of human faculties, feelings, and activities, though we are bound to suppose that in the divine nature they exist in an infinitely higher degree, than the corresponding faculties, feelings, and activities of man. In short, by a God I mean a beneficent supernatural spirit, the ruler of the world or of some part of it, who resembles man in nature though he excels him in knowledge, goodness, and power. This is, I think, the sense in which the ordinary man speaks of a God, and I believe that he is right in so doing. I am aware that it has been not unusual, especially of late years, to apply the name of God to very different conceptions, to empty it of all implications of personality, and to reduce it to signifying something very large and very vague, such as the Infinite or the Absolute (whatever these hard words may signify) the great First Cause, the Universal Substance, the stream of tendency by which all things seek to fulfill the law of their being, and so forth. Now, without expressing opinion as to the truth or falsehood of the views implied by such applications of the name of God, I cannot but regard them as illegitimate extensions of the term, in short, an abuse of language, and I venture to protest against it in the interest, not only of verbal accuracy, but of clear thinking, because it is apt to conceal from ourselves and others a real and very important change of thought; in particular it may lead many to imagine that the persons who use the name of God in one or other of these extended senses retain theological opinions which they may in fact have long abandoned. Thus the misuse of the name of God may resemble the stratagem in war of putting up dummies to make an enemy imagine that a fort is still held long after it has been abandoned by the garrison. (*The Belief in Immortality*; pp. 9-10. Vol. I.).

This expression of opinion from an authoritative quarter is very much needed. The fear of public opinion displayed by many "advanced" thinkers is in this country one of the greatest obstacles to rapid advance. It is simply deplorable to observe the trouble taken by some to coin new names, or the illegitimate use made of old ones, for no other discoverable reason than that of disguising from the world the fact that the orthodox beliefs are no longer held. The need of to-day is not so much liberal thought as strong and courageous thought; and one would cheerfully hand back to orthodoxy a fairly large parcel of a certain type of heretical thinker in exchange for a single one who used plain language to express clear convictions.

What is it that the mass of believers have in their minds when they speak of God? There can be no doubt but that what the plain man has always understood by "God" is a person. Every book of religious devotion implies this; every prayer that is offered takes it for granted that *someone* will listen, and probably grant the petition. God is personal, God is just, God is beneficent, God is intelligent, these are conceptions that are bound up with all the religions of the world, and without which they would lack both significance and value. A very acute theistic writer, Mr. W. H. Mallock, puts this quite plainly when he says that the God of theism "is represented as revealing himself in the universe, firstly, as the mind which animates and moves everything, secondly, as a purposing mind which is infinitely wise and powerful, and has created a perfect universe with a view to some perfect end; and lastly, as an ethical mind which out of all the things created by it, has selected men as the object of a preferential love. A personality which thinks and wills and loves and hates. That is what mankind in the mass have always meant by 'God.'"

Indeed, any other kind of God is inconceivable. Whatever may be the metaphysical subtleties employed, we come ultimately to that. It is this, the older and the vital conception that is being fought for. The arguments for any other kind of existence are mere subterfuges. The pleas for an "Absolute" or an "Unconditioned" are only used to buttress the older conception, and never till the older one has lost its force. The unconditioned God is argued for only that it may serve as the basis for the belief in a personal one. What is proved is not what is asked for; what is asked for is not what is proved. No wonder that so eminent a writer as Mr. F. H. Bradley feels constrained to give these verbalistic thimble riggers a smart rap over the knuckles, as in the following passage:—

Most of those who insist on the "personality of God" are intellectually dishonest. They desire one conclusion, and, to reach it, they argue for another. But the second, if proved, is quite different, and answers their purpose only because they obscure it and confound it with the first.... The deity they want, is, of course, finite, a person much like themselves, with thoughts and feelings limited and mutable in the process of time.... And for their purpose, what is not this is really nothing. (*Appearance and Reality*; p. 532).

10

And it is really what people mean by God that is decisive. It is not at all a question of what they might be made to mean, or what they ought to mean. It is wholly a matter of what they *do* mean. And to say that what people intend to affirm in an expression of belief is not true, is to say that the belief itself is false. If the God I believe in is a delusion, then my God ceases to exist. True, I may if I think it worth while acquire another one, but that will not revive the first. It is what people believe that is the important question, not what some ingenious speculator may succeed in making the belief stand for.

Honestly to be of service to theism the God established must be a person. To be intelligible, having regard to the historical developments of religion, the God proved must be a person. The relation demanded by religion between man and God must be of a personal character. No man can love a pure abstraction; he might as reasonably fall in love with a triangle or profess devotion to the equator. The God of religion must be a person, and it is precisely that, as a controlling force of the universe, in which modern thought finds it more and more difficult to believe, and which modern science decisively rejects. And in rejecting this the death blow is given to those religious ideas, which however disguised find their origin in the fear-stricken ignorance of the primitive savage.

Chapter II

The Origin of the Idea of God

The alleged universality of the belief in God is only inferentially an argument for its truth. The inference is that if men have everywhere developed a particular belief, this general agreement could only have been reached as a consequence of a general experience. A universal effect implies a universal cause. So put the argument seems impressive. As a matter of fact the statement is one long tissue of fallacies and unwarranted assumptions.

In the first place, even admitting the universal pressure of certain facts, it by no means follows that the theistic interpretation of those facts is the only one admissible. There is no exception to the fact that men have everywhere come to the conclusion that the earth was flat, and yet a wider and truer knowledge proved that universal belief to be quite false. The fact of a certain belief being universal only warrants the assumption that the belief itself has a cause, but it tells us nothing whatever concerning its truthfulness. The truth here is that the argument from universality dates its origin from a stage of human culture suitable to the god idea itself, a stage when very little was known concerning the workings of the mind or the laws of mental development. Otherwise it would have been seen that all the universality of a belief really proves is the universality of the human mind—and that means that, given an organism of a certain kind, it will react in substantially an identical manner to the same stimuli. Thus it is not surprising to find that as the human organism is everywhere fundamentally alike, it has everywhere come to the same conclusions in face of the same set of conditions. A man reacts to the universe in one way, and a jelly fish in another way. And universality is as true of the reactions of the latter as it is of those of the former.

And this means that a delusion may be as widespread as truth, a false inference may gain as general an acceptance as a true one. What belief has been more general than the belief in witches, fairies, and the like? But we see in the prevalence of these and similar beliefs, not a presumption of their truth, but only the grounds for a search after the conditions, social and psychological, which gave them birth.

The truth is that the conditions which give rise to the belief in gods are found in all ages, and no one would be more surprised than the Atheist to find it otherwise. But here, precisely as in the case of good and bad spirits, the vital question is not that people have everywhere believed in the existence of supernatural beings,[1] but an understanding of the

---

[1] Both the words "supernatural" and "God" are here used somewhat loosely. In fact the conception of the supernatural arises gradually, and as a consequence of developing knowledge which, so to speak, splits the universe into two. So also with the belief in God. There is clearly an earlier form in which there exists a kind of mental plasma from which the more definite conception of God is subsequently formed. On this topic the reader may consult "The Threshold of Religion," by R. R. Marett, 1914.

conditions from which the beliefs themselves have grown. That alone can determine whether in studying the god idea we are studying the acquisition of a truth or the growth of a fallacy.

Next, while it may be granted, at least provisionally, that the belief in supernatural beings is universal, against that has to be set the fact that the whole tendency of social development is to narrow the range of the belief, to restrict the scope of its authority, and to so attenuate it that it becomes of no value precisely where it is supposed to be of most use. The belief in God is least questioned where civilization is lowest; it is called into the most serious question where civilization is most advanced. To-day the belief in God is only universal in the sense that some representatives of it are to be found in all societies. The majority may still profess to have it, but it has ceased to be universal in the strict sense of the term. Nor will it be disputed that the number of convinced disbelievers is everywhere on the increase. The fact is everywhere lamented by the official exponents of religion. All that we can say is that the belief in God is universal—with those who believe in him. And even here universality of belief is only secured by their refraining from discussing precisely what it is they mean by "God," and what it is they believe in. There is agreement in obscurity, each one dreading to see clearly the features of his assumed friend for fear he should recognize the face of an enemy.

Finally, the suspicious feature must be pointed out that the belief in God owes its existence, not to the trained and educated observation of civilized times, but to the uncritical reflection of the primitive mind. It has its origin there, and it would indeed be remarkable if, while in almost every other direction the primitive mind showed itself to be hopelessly wrong, in its interpretation of the world in this particular respect it has proved itself to be altogether right. As a matter of

14

fact, this primitive assumption is going the way of the others, the only difference being that it is passing through more phases than some. But the decay is plain to all save those who refuse to see. The process of refinement cannot go on for ever. In other matters knowledge passes from a nebulous and indefinite stage to a precise and definite one. In the case of theism it pursues an opposite course. From the very definite god, or gods, of primitive mankind we advance to the vague and indefinite god of the modern theist—a God who, apparently, means nothing and does nothing, and at most stands as a symbol for our irremovable ignorance. Clearly this process cannot go on for ever. The work of attenuation must stop at some point. And one may safely predict that just as the advance of scientific knowledge has taken over one department after another that was formerly regarded as within the province of religion, so one day it will be borne in upon all that an hypothesis such as that of theism, which does nothing and explains nothing, may be profitably dispensed with.

What really remains for discussion is a problem of socio-psychology. That is, we have to determine the conditions of origin of so widespread a belief, but which we believe to be false. The materials for answering this question are now at our command, and whatever differences of opinion there may be concerning the stages of development, there is very little concerning their essential character. And it is not without significance that this question of origin is one that the present-day apologists of theism seem pretty unanimous in leaving severely alone.

Let us commence with the fact that religion is something that is acquired. Every work on the origin of religion assumes it, and all investigation warrants the assumption. The question at issue is the mode of acquisition. And here one word of caution is advisable. The wide range of religious ideas and their existence at a very low culture stage, precludes the assumption that religious ideas are generated in the same conscious way as are scientific theories. Even with the modern mind our conclusions concerning many of the affairs of life are formed in a semi-conscious manner. Most frequently they are generated subconsciously, and are only consciously formulated under pressure of circumstances. And if we are to understand religion aright we must be on our guard against attributing to primitive mankind a degree of scientific curiosity and reflective power to which it can lay no claim. We have to allow for what one writer well calls "physiological thought," thought, that is, which rises subconsciously and has its origin in the pressure of insistent experience.

A comprehensive survey of religious beliefs show that there are only two things that can be said to be common to them all. They differ in teachings, in their conceptions of deity, and in modes of worship. But all religions agree in believing in some kind of ghostly existence and in a continued life beyond the grave. I use the expression, "ghostly existence," because we can really trace the idea of God backward until we lose the definite figure in a very general conception, much as astronomers have taught us to lose a definite world in the primitive fire-mist. So when we get beyond the culture stage at which we meet with the definite man-like God, we encounter an indefinite thought stage at which we can dimly mark the existence of a frame of mind that was to give birth to the more concrete conception.

The most general term for the belief in the various orders of gods thus becomes the belief in invisible, super-material beings, like, and yet superior to man. It is for this reason that Professor Tylor's definition of religion as "the belief in spiritual beings—so long as we do not use the term "spiritual" in its modern sense"—seems to me the moat satisfactory definition yet offered. It is the one point on which all religions agree, and for this reason may be regarded as their essential feature.

This taken for granted, our next point of enquiry is, What was there in the conditions of primitive life that would give rise to a belief in this super-material, or in modern language, spiritual existence? Now there are at least two sets of experiences that seem adequate to the required explanation. The one is normal, the other abnormal. The first is connected directly with the universal experience of dreams. The savage is, as Tylor says, a severely practical person. He believes what he sees and, one may add, he sees what he believes. Knowing nothing of the distinction we draw between a fact and an illusion, ignorant of the functions, or even the existence of a nervous system, the dreams of a savage are to him as real as his waking experiences. He does not say "I dreamed I saw So-So," but like the Biblical characters he says, "I saw So-So in a dream." The two forms of expression carry all the difference between fact and fancy. One thing is therefore obvious to the savage mind — something escapes from the body, travels about, and returns. Such a conviction does not represent the conclusions of a genius speculating upon the meaning of unexplained facts. It is a conviction steadily built up by the pressure of unvarying experience, as steadily as is the conviction that fire burns or that water is wet. The very universality of the belief is proof that it had some such sub-conscious origin.

A second class of experiences lead to the same conclusion. In temporary loss of consciousness the savage again sees proof of the existence of a double. With epilepsy or insanity there is offered decisive proof that some spirit has taken possession of the individual's body. Even in civilized countries this belief was widely held hardly more than a century ago. And both these classes of experience are enforced by the belief that the shadow of a man, an echo, a reflection seen in water, etc., are all real things. The proofs that the belief in a "soul" does originate in this way are now so plentiful that exact references are needless. Examination of primitive religious beliefs all over the world yield the one result, without there being any evidence to the contrary.

Primitive philosophy does not stop here. Man dreams of things as well as of persons, and a general extension of the belief in a ghost or double is made until it covers almost everything. As Tylor says, "the doctrine of souls is worked out with remarkable breadth and consistency. The souls of animals are recognized by a natural extension from the theory of human souls; the souls of trees and plants follow in some vague partial way; and the souls of inanimate objects expand the category to the extremist boundary." The reasoning of the primitive mind is thus, given its limitations and unsound premises, uncompromisingly logical. One can trace the processes of reasoning more easily than is the case with modern man because it is less disturbed by cross-currents of acquired knowledge and conflicting interests.

I am giving but the barest outline of a vast subject because I am desirous of keeping the attention of the reader on what I believe to be the main issue. For that reason I am not discussing whether animism—the vitalizing of inanimate objects—has an independent origin, or whether it is a mere extension of the ghost theory. Either theory does not affect my main position, which is that the idea of God is derived from the ignorance of primitive humanity, and has no other authority than a misunderstanding of natural facts. On that point the agreement among all schools of anthropologists is now very general. Personally, however, I do not believe that men would ever have given a soul to trees or other natural objects unless they had first given them to living beings, and had thus familiarized themselves with the conception of a double.

At present, though, we are on the track of the gods. The belief that every human being, and nearly every object, possesses a soul, ends in surrounding man with a cloud of spirits against which he has to be always on his guard. The general situation is well put by Miss Kingsley, who gives a picture of the West African that may well stand for the savage world in general.

Everything happens by the action of spirits. The thing he does himself is done by the spirit within acting on his body, the matter with which that spirit is associated. Everything that is done by other things is done by their spirit associated with their particular mass of matter.... The native will point out to you a lightning stricken tree and tell you its spirit has been killed. He will tell you, when the earthen cooking pot is broken, it has lost its spirit. If his weapon failed him, it is because he has stolen or made its spirit sick by means of his influence on other spirits of the same class.... In every action of his life he shows you how he lives with a great, powerful spirit world around him. You see him before running out to hunt or fight rubbing stuff in his weapon to strengthen the spirit that is in it; telling it the while what care he has taken of it; running through a list of what he had given it before, though these things had been hard to give; and begging it, in the hour of his dire necessity, not to fail him.... You see him bending over the face of the river, talking to its spirit with proper incantations, asking it when it meets an enemy to upset his canoe and destroy him ... or, as I have myself seen in Congo Française, to take down with it, away from his village, the pestilence of the spotted death. (*West African Studies*; pp. 394-5).

When Feurbach said that the "realm of memory was the world of souls," he expressed a profound truth in a striking manner. It is dreams, swoons, catalepsy, with their allied states which suggest the existence of a double or ghost. Even in the absence of the mass of evidence from all quarters in support of this, the

19

fact of the ghost always being pictured as identical in clothing and figure with the dead man would be almost enough to demonstrate its dream origin. Into that aspect of the matter, however, we do not now intend to enter. We are now only concerned with the bearing of the ghost theory on the origin of God. Another step or two and we shall have reached that point. Believing himself surrounded on all sides by a world of ghosts the great concern of the savage is to escape their ill-will or to secure their favor. Affection and fear—fear that the ghost, if his wants are neglected, will wreak vengeance through the agency of disease, famine, or accident—leads insensibly to the ghosts of one's relations becoming objects of veneration, propitiation, and petition. All ghosts receive some attention for a certain time after death, but naturally special and sustained honors are reserved for the heads of families,[2] and for such as have been distinguished for various qualities during life. In this way ancestor worship becomes one of the most general forms of religious observances, and the gradual development of the great man or the deceased ancestor into a deity follows by easy stages. The principles of ancestor worship, to again cite the indispensible Tylor, are not difficult to understand:—

They plainly keep up the social relations of the living world. The dead ancestor, now passed into a deity, simply goes on protecting: his own family and receiving suit and service from them as of old; the dead chief still watches over his own tribe, still holds his authority by helping friends and harming enemies, still rewards the right and sharply punishes the wrong.

That this deification of ancestors and of dead men actually takes place is indisputable. The Mythologies of Greece and

---

[2] For the importance of this in the history of religion see Fustel de Coulanges' "The Ancient City."

Rome offer numerous examples, and the deification of the Roman Emperors became the regular rule. Numerous examples to the same end are supplied from India by Mr. W. Crookes and Sir A. C. Lyall. That this way of honoring the dead is not limited to natives is shown by the famous case of General Nicholson, who actually received the honor of deification during his lifetime. Anyone who cares to consult those storehouses of information, Spencer's "Principles of Sociology" (Vol. I.), Tylor's "Primitive Culture," and Frazer's "Golden Bough" will find the whole god-making process set forth with a wealth of illustration that can hardly fail to carry conviction. Finally, in the case of Japan and China we have living examples of an organized system of religion based upon the deification of ancestors.[3]

It will make it easier to understand the evolution of the god from the ghost if we bear in mind that with primitive man the gods are conceived neither as independent existences nor as creators. Even immortality is not asserted of them. The modern notions of deity, largely due to the attempt to accommodate the idea of god to certain metaphysical and philosophical conceptions, are so intermingled with the primitive idea, that there is always the danger of reading into the primitive intelligence more than was ever there. The consequence is that by confusing the two senses of the word many find it difficult to realize how one has grown out of the other. Such ideas as

---

[3] The perpetuation of this earlier stage of religion in China and Japan appears to make the transition to Free-thought easier than in countries where religion has under-gone a more advanced evolution. In both the countries named, the better minds find it quite easy to treat their religion as merely the respect paid to ancestors, and thus divest it of the supernatural element. In Christian countries there is also the attempt to restate beliefs in terms of current morality and sociology, but the transition is more difficult.

those of creation and independence are quite foreign to the primitive mind. Savages are like children in this respect; their interest in things is primarily of a practical character. A child does not begin by asking how a thing came to be; it asks what it is for or what it does. So the prime concern of the savage is, what are certain things for? what will they do? are they injurious or beneficial? It is because of this practical turn of mind that so much attention is paid to the ghost, having once accepted its existence as a fact. The superiority of the gods do not consist in their substantial difference from himself, but in the greater power for good or evil conferred upon them by their invisible existence. Creation is a conception that does not arise until the capacity for philosophical speculation has developed. Then reflection sets to work; the nature of the god undergoes modification, and the long process of accommodating primitive religious beliefs to later knowledge commences, the end of which we have not yet seen.

The process of reading modern speculations into the religion of the savage leads to some curious results, one of which we cannot forbear mentioning. In his little work on "Animism" Mr. Edward Clodd, after tracing the fundamental ideas of religion to primitive delusion, says: —

Herein (*i.e.*, in dream and visions) are to be found the sufficing materials for a belief in an entity in the body, but not of it, which can depart and return at will, and which man everywhere has more or less vaguely envisaged as his "double" or "other self."... The distinction between soul and body, which explained to man his own actions, was the key to the actions of animate and inanimate things. A personal life and will controlled them. This was obviously brought home to him more forcibly in the actions of living things, since these so closely resembled his own that he saw no difference between themselves and him. *Not in this matter alone have the intuitions of the savage found their confirmation in the discoveries of modern science....* Ignorant of the reflection of sound, how else could he account for the echoes flung back from the hillside? Ignorant of the law of the interruption of light, how else could he explain the advancing and retreating shadows? *In some sense they must be alive; an inference supported by modern science.*

The italics in the above passages are mine, and they serve to illustrate how certain writers manage to introduce quite misleading conceptions to their readers. It almost causes one to cease wondering at the persistence of religion when one finds a writer accepting the results of anthropological research, and at the same time claiming that savage "intuitions" are confirmed by modern science. If that be true, then all that Mr. Clodd has previously written must be dismissed as untrue. The statement is, however, quite inaccurate. The inference drawn by the savage is not supported by modern science. Neither on the existence of a soul nor on the existence of a god, nor on the nature of disease, nor on the causes of physical or psychical states has science confirmed the "intuitions" (whatever that conveniently cloudy word may mean) of the primitive savage. The acquisition of correct views would indeed be an easy thing if they could be gained by the "intuitions" of an untaught savage.

The assertion that "in some sense" natural forces must be alive (as though there can be any real sense in a term except the right sense), and that this inference is "supported by modern physics," is an illustration of that playing with words which is fatal to exact thought. The only sense in which the expression is used in physics is that of "active," and both "active" and "alive" owe their vogue to the necessity for controverting the older view that natural forces are "inert" or "dead" and need some external force to produce anything. It is a mere figure of speech; the evil is when it is taken and used as an exact

23

expression of scientific fact. Let a reader of Mr. Clodd ask himself whether the life he thinks of when he speaks of forces being alive is animal life, and he will at once see the absurdity of the statement. And if he does not mean animal life, what life does he mean?

Putting on one side all such attempts at accommodation, we may safely say that given the origin of religion in the manner indicated, one may trace—at least in outline—the development of religion from the primitive ghost worship up to the rituals and beliefs of current creeds. I do not mean by this that *all* religious beliefs and practices spring directly from ghost worship. Once religion is established, and the myth-making capacity let loose, additions are made that are due to all sorts of causes. The Romans and Greeks, for example, seem to have created a number of deities out of pure abstractions—gods of peace, of war, of fortune, and so forth. Why particular deities were invented, and how they became attached to particular groups of phenomena, are questions that it is often impossible to answer with any great degree of certainty, but why there should be any gods at all is a question that can be answered, I think, on the lines above indicated.

The way in which the primitive ghost worship probably paved the way for some of the doctrines of the "higher" religions may be seen on taking a story such as the death and resurrection of the Gospel Jesus. In his treatise on "The Attis" Mr. Grant Allen made the ingenious suggestion that the greater fertility of the ground on and near the grave, owing to the food placed there to feed the ghost, would produce in the savage mind the conviction that this increased fertility was due to the beneficent activity of the double of the dead man. Reasoning from this basis, it would be a simple conclusion that the production, or lack, of crops was everywhere due to the action of good or evil spirits. In the next place, it must be remembered that it is the

24

act of dying which raises the human being to the level of a guardian spirit or god; and from this to the production of a god by ceremonial killing would be a natural and an easy step. In this last respect, at least, we are upon the firm ground of fact, and not on that of mere theory. If a reader will take the trouble to peruse the numerous examples collected by Tylor in the first chapter of his "Primitive Culture," and those provided by Frazer in the "Golden Bough," he will find the evidence for this overwhelming. Examples of the practice of killing a human being and burying his body under the foundations of a castle or a bridge are very common, and the modern custom of burying coins under a foundation-stone is a harmless and interesting survival of this custom. In some parts of Africa a boy and girl are buried where a village is to be established. In Polynesia the central pillar of a temple was placed on the body of a human victim. In Scotland there is the legend that St. Columba buried the body of St. Oran under his monastery to make the building secure. Any country will supply stories of a similar kind. Finally, we have the amusing story of the manner in which Sir Richard Burton narrowly escaped deification. Exploring in Afghanistan in the disguise of a Mohammedan fakir, he received a friendly hint that he would do well to get off without delay. He expressed surprise, as the people seemed very fond of him. That, it was explained, was the cause of the trouble. They thought so much of him they intended to kill him, and thus retain so excellent a man with them for ever.

When Tylor wrote, the prevalent impression was that this killing of human beings was due to a desire to appease the spirits of the place. Later investigation showed that instead of a sacrifice it was a creation. The purpose was to create a local god who would watch over the building or settlement. God-making was thus shown to be a universal practice.

Our next step must be taken in the company of Sir James Frazer. On all-fours with the practice of creating a guardian deity for a building is that of making a similar guardian for crops and vegetation. The details of this practice are interesting, but they need not now detain us. It is enough that the practice existed, and, as Frazer shows, was an annual practice. Year by year the god was killed in order that the seed might ripen and the harvest be secured. In some cases the body was cut up and pieces buried in the fields; in other cases it was burned and the ashes scattered over the ground. Gradually the ritual becomes more elaborate, but the central idea remains intact that of a human being converted into a god by being killed, a man sacrificed for the benefit of the tribe. In the light of these researches the New Testament story becomes only a more recent version of a widespread savage superstition. The time of the sacrifice, the symbolism, the practices all prove this. The crucified Savior, in honor of whom all the Christian cathedrals and churches of the world are built, is only another late survival of the god-making practice of primitive savagery.

The gods are, then, ultimately deified ghosts. They are born of misinterpreted subjective and objective experiences. This is among the surest and most firmly established results of modern investigation. It matters not what modifications later knowledge may demand; it will only mean a change of form, not of substance. On any scientific theory we are bound to explain the origin of the gods in terms of human error. And no subsequent development can alter its character. We may trace the various stages of a universal delusion, but nothing can convert a delusion into a reality. It is now universally recognized that the primitive notions of gods represent false conclusions from misunderstood facts. No one now believes that the visions seen during sleep are proofs of a wandering double. No one believes that it is necessary to supply the ghost of the dead with food, or with weapons, or with wives. We do not believe that the wind, the stars, the waters are alive or are capable of being influenced by our petitions. All the phenomena upon which the god idea was originally built are now known to be susceptible to a radically different explanation. And if this is so, what other foundations have we on which to build a belief in God? There is none. There is only one plausible reason for the belief in God, and that is the reason advanced by the savage. When we get beyond that we are not dealing with reasons for holding the belief, but only with excuses for retaining it. Unfortunately, thousands are familiar with the excuses, and only a few with the reasons. Were it otherwise a great deal of what follows need never have been written.

Chapter III

Have we a Religious Sense?

In all discussions of theism there is one point that is usually overlooked. This is that theism is in the nature of a hypothesis. And, like every hypothesis, its value is proportionate to the extent to which it offers a satisfactory explanation of the facts with which it professes to deal. If it can offer no explanation its value is nil. If its explanation is only partial, its value will be determined by the degree to which it can claim superiority over any other hypothesis that is before us. But every hypothesis implies two things. There is a group of things to be explained, and there is the hypothesis itself that is offered in explanation. In the harmony of the two, and in the possibility of verification, lies the only proof of truth that can be offered.

If this be granted it at once disposes of the plea that a conviction of the existence of God springs from some special quality of the mind which enables man to arrive at a conclusion in a manner different from the way in which conclusions concerning other subjects are reached. Intuition as a method of discovering truth is pure delusion. All that can be rationally meant by such a word as intuition is summarized experience. When we speak of knowing a thing "intuitively," all that we can mean is that, experience having furnished us with a

28

sufficient guidance, we are able to reach a conclusion so rapidly that we cannot follow the steps of the mental process involved. That this is so is seen in the fact that our intuitions always follow the line of our experience. A stockbroker may "intuitively" foresee a rise or fall of the market, but his intuition will fail him when considering the possibilities of a chemical composition. To say that a man knows a thing by intuition is only one way of saying that he does not know how he knows it—that is, he is unable to trace the stages of his own mental operations. And in this sense intuition is universal. It belongs as much to the cooking of a dumpling as it does to the belief in deity.

But it is evident that when the theist talks of intuition, what he has in mind is something very different from this. He is thinking of some special quality of mind that operates independently of experience, either racial or individual. And this simply does not exist. In religion man is never putting into operation qualities of mind different from those he employs in other directions. Whether we call a state of mind religious or not is determined, not by the mental processes involved, but by the object to which it is directed. Hatred and love, anger, pleasure, awe, curiosity, reverence, even worship, are exactly the same whether directed towards "God" or towards anything else. Human qualities are fundamentally identical, and may be expressed in relation to all sorts of objects.

The attempt to mark religion off from the rest of life, to be approached by special methods and in a special frame of mind, takes many forms, and it may be illustrated by the manner in which it is dealt with by Professor Arthur Thomson. In a little work entitled "An Introduction to Science," and specially intended for general consumption, he remarks, as a piece of advice to his readers:—

We would remind ourselves and our readers that the whole subject should be treated with reverence and sympathy, for it is hardly possible to exaggerate the huge role of religion in human life. Whatever be our views, we must recognize that just as the great mathematicians and metaphysicians represent the aristocracy of the human intellect, so the great religious geniuses represent the aristocracy of human emotion. And in this connection it is probably useful to bear in mind that in all discussions about religious ideas or feelings we should ourselves be in an exalted mood, and yet "with a compelling sense of our own limitations," and of the vastness and mysteriousness of the world.

If Professor Thomson had been writing on "Frames of Mind Fatal to Scientific Investigation" he could hardly have chosen a better illustration of his thesis. One may safely say that anyone who started an examination of religion in this spirit, and maintained it throughout his examination, would perform something little short of a miracle did he reach a sound conclusion. A feeling of sympathy may pass, but why "reverence"? Reverence is a very complex state, but it certainly includes respect and a certain measure of affection. And how is one to rationally have respect or affection for anything *before* one has ascertained that they are deserving of either? Is anyone who happens to believe that religion is *not* worthy of reverence to be ruled out as being unfit to express an opinion? Clearly, on this rule, either we compel a man to sacrifice his sense of self-respect before we will allow him to be heard, or we pack the jury with persons who confess to have reached a decision before they have heard the evidence. It would almost seem from the expression that while examining religion we should be in an "exalted mood" that Professor Thomson has in view the last contingency. For by an exalted mood we can only understand a religious mood—that is, we must believe in religion before we examine it, otherwise our examination is

30

profanity. Well, that is just the cry of the priest in all ages. And while it is sound religion, there is no question of its being shocking science. Even the mere feeling of exaltation is not to be encouraged during a scientific investigation. One can understand Kepler when he had discovered the true laws of planetary motion, or Newton when he embraced in one magnificent generalization the fall of a stone and the revolution of a planet, experiencing a feeling of exaltation; but exaltation must follow, not precede, the conclusion. At any rate, there are few scientific teachers who would encourage such a feeling during investigation.

Leaving for a moment the question of religious geniuses being the aristocrats of human emotion, we may take the same writer's view of the limitations of science, thus providing an opening for the intrusion of religion. This is given in the form of a criticism of the following well-known passage from Huxley:—

If the fundamental proposition of evolution is true, namely, that the entire world, animate and inanimate, is the result of the mutual interaction, according to definite laws, of forces possessed by the molecules which made up the primitive nebulosity of the universe; then it is no less certain that the present actual world reposed potentially in the cosmic vapor, and that an intelligence, if great enough, could from his knowledge of the properties of the molecules of that vapor have predicted the state of the fauna in Great Britain in 1888 with as much certitude as we say what will happen to the vapor of our breath on a cold day in winter.

Now, if the principle of evolution be accepted, the truth of Huxley's statement appears to be self-evident. It may be that no intelligence capable of making such a calculation will ever exist, but the abstract possibility remains. Professor Thomson

31

calls it "a very strong and confident statement," which illustrates the need for philosophical criticism. His criticism of Huxley's statement is based on two grounds. These are: (1) "No complete physico-chemical description has ever been given of any distinctively vital activity; and (2) the physical description of things cannot cover biological phenomena, nor can the biological description cover mental and moral phenomena." There is, he says,

The physical order of nature—the inorganic world—where mechanism reigns supreme. (2) There is the vital order of nature—the world of organisms—where mechanism proves insufficient. (3) There is the physical order of nature—the world of mind—where mechanism is irrelevant. Thus there are three fundamental sciences—Physics, Biology, and Psychology—each with characteristic questions, categories and formulas.

Now, however earnestly Huxley's statement calls for criticism, it is clear to us that nothing useful in that direction is offered by Prof. Thomson. It is quite plain that the abstract possibility of such a calculation as that named by Huxley can never be ruled out by science, since such a conception lies at the root of all scientific thinking. After all, want of knowledge only proves— want of knowledge; and Sir Oliver Lodge would warn Prof. Thomson of the extreme danger of resting an argument on the ignorance of science at any particular time.[4]

---

[4] "The present powerlessness of science to explain or originate life is a convenient weapon wherewith to fell a pseudo-scientific antagonist who is dogmatizing too loudly out of bounds; but it is not perfectly secure as a permanent support.... Life in its ultimate elements and on its material side is such a simple thing, it is but a slight extension of known chemical and physical forces.... I apprehend that there is not a

I note this statement of Professor Thomson's chiefly because it illustrates a very common method of dealing with the mechanistic or non-theistic view of the universe. In this matter Professor Thomson may claim the companionship of Sir Oliver Lodge, who says, "Materialism is appropriate to the material world, not as a philosophy, but as a working creed, as a proximate, an immediate formula for guiding research. Everything beyond that belongs to another region, and must be reached by other methods. To explain the psychical in terms of physics and chemistry is simply impossible.... The extreme school of biologists ... ought to say, if they were consistent, there is nothing but physics and chemistry at work anywhere." With both these writers there is the common assumption that the mechanist assumes there is a physical and chemical explanation of all phenomena. And the assumption is false. There is a story of a well-known lecturer on physiology who commenced an address on the stomach by remarking that that organ had been called this, that, and the other, but the one thing he wished his students to bear in mind was that it was a stomach. So the mechanist, while firmly believing that there is an ascending unity in all natural phenomena, is never silly enough to deny that living things are alive, or that thinking beings think.

But unless Professor Thomson does impute this to the mechanist, we quite fail to see the relevance his assertion that there are three departments, physics, biology, and psychology, each with its characteristic questions, categories, and formulas. Of course, there are, and equally, of course, physical laws will not cover biological facts; nor will biological laws cover

---

biologist but believes (perhaps quite erroneously) that sooner or later the discovery will be made, and that a cell discharging all the essential functions of life will be constructed out of inorganic material." ("Man and the Universe," Chap. I.).

33

psychological ones. This is not due to any occult cause, but to the simple fact that as each group of phenomena has its characteristic features, each set of laws are framed to cover the phenomena presented by that group. Otherwise there would be no need of these special laws. It is astonishing how paralyzing is the effect of the theistic obsession on the minds of even scientific men, since it leads them to ignore what is really a basic consideration in scientific method.

Perhaps a word or two more on this topic is advisable. If it is permissible to arrange natural phenomena in a serial order, we may place them in succession as physical, chemical, biological, and psychological. But these names represent no more than descriptions of certain features that are to the group common, otherwise the grouping would be useless and impossible. And it is part of the business of science to frame "laws"—descriptions—of phenomena such as will enable us to express their characteristic features in a brief formula. It is, therefore, quite true to say that you cannot express vital phenomena in terms of physics or chemistry. And no materialist who took the trouble to understand materialism, instead of taking a statement of what it is from an anti-materialist, ever thought otherwise. *Each specific group of phenomena can only be covered by laws that belong to that group, and which were framed for that express purpose.* A psychological fact can no more be expressed in terms of chemistry than a physical fact can be expressed in terms of biology. These truths are as plain to the mechanist as they are to the vitalist. Mental life, the scientific categories, are real to all; the only question at issue is that of their origin.

To explain is to make intelligible, and in that sense all scientific explanation consists in the establishing of equivalents. When we say that A, B, C are the factors of D, we have asserted D is the equivalent of A, B, C—plus, of course, all that results from the combination of the factors. When we say that we have explained the formation of water by showing it to be the product of H.2.O. we have shown that whether we say "water" or use the chemical formula we are making identical statements. If we are working out a problem in dynamics we meet with exactly the same principle. We must prove that the resultant accounts for all the forces in operation at the time. Now, all that the mechanist claims is that it is extremely probable that one day the scientist will be able to work out the exact physico-chemical conditions that are the equivalents of biological phenomena, and, in turn, the physico-chemical-biological conditions that are the equivalents of psychological phenomena. Very considerable progress has already been made in this direction, and, as Sir Oliver Lodge says, there are probably very few scientific men who would deny the likelihood of this being done.

But this does not deny the existence of differences between these groups of phenomena; neither does it assert that we can describe the characteristic features of one group in terms that belong to another group. Once a group of phenomena, biological, or chemical is there, we must have special formulas to describe them, otherwise there would be no need for these divisions. It is admitted that the earth was at one time destitute of life; it is also admitted that there are forms of life destitute of those features which we call mind. And, whatever be their mode of origin, once introduced they must be dealt with in special terms. Psychological facts must be expressed in terms of psychology, biological facts in terms of biology, and chemical facts in terms of chemistry. You may give the chemical and physical equivalent of a sunset. That is one aspect. You may also give the psychological explanation of the emotion of man on beholding it. That is another aspect. But you cannot express the psychological fact in terms of chemistry because it belongs to quite another category. A psychological fact, as such, is ultimate. So is a chemical or a biological fact. If by analysis you reduce the psychological fact to its chemical and biological equivalents, its character as a psychological fact is destroyed. That is the product of the synthesis, and to seek in analysis for what only exists in synthesis, is surely to altogether misunderstand the spirit of scientific method. The curious thing is that a mere layman should have to correct men of science on this matter.

We can now return to Prof. Thomson's attempt to claim for religion a special place in the sphere of emotion. He claims, in the passage already cited, that "as the great mathematicians and metaphysicians represent the aristocracy of human intellect so the great religious geniuses represent the aristocracy of human emotion." There is nothing new in this claim, neither is there any evidence of its truth. Coleridge's dictum that the proper antithesis to religion is poetry is open to serious objection, but there is more to be said for it than may be said for the antithesis set up by Prof. Thomson. As a matter of fact, religious geniuses have often pursued their work with as much attention to scientific precision as was possible, and have prided themselves that they made no appeal to mere emotion. Justification by emotion has only been attempted when other means of securing conviction has failed. And the appeal to emotion has become popular for very obvious reasons. It enables the ordinary theologian to feel a comfortable superiority over a Spencer or a Darwin. It enables mediocrities to enjoy the feeling of being wise without the trouble of acquiring wisdom. It enables inherited prejudices to rank as reasoned convictions. And, in addition, there is nothing that cannot be conveniently proved or disproved by such a method.

In whatever form the distinction is met with it harbors a fallacy. Intellectual activity is not and cannot be divorced from emotion. There are states of mind in which feeling predominates, and there are others in which reason

36

predominates. But all intellectual states involve a feeling element. The often-made remark that feeling and intellect are in conflict is true only in the sense that ultimately certain intellectual states, *plus* their associated feelings, are in conflict with other intellectual states plus *their* associated feelings. To realize this one need only consider the sheer pleasure that results from the rapid sweep of the mind through a lengthy chain of reasoning, and the positive pain that ensues when the terms of a proposition baffles comprehension. The force of this is admitted by Prof. Thomson in the remark that man at the limit of his endeavor has fallen back on religion. Quite so; that is the painful feelings evoked by an intellectual failure have thrown a certain type of mind back on religion. In this they have acted like one who flies to a drug for relief from a pain he lacks the courage to bear. They take a narcotic when, often enough, the real need is for a stimulant.

In sober truth religion is no more necessarily connected with the emotions than are other subjects of investigation. Those who have made the pursuit of "cold scientific truth" their life's work have shown every whit as much ardor and passion as those who have given their life to religion. The picture of man sacrificing himself in the cause of religion is easily matched by a Vesalius haunting the charnel houses of Europe, and risking the most loathsome diseases in the interests of scientific research. The abiding passion for truth in a character such as that of Roger Bacon or Bruno easily matches the enthusiasm of the missionary monk. The passion and the enthusiasm for science is less advertised than the passion and the enthusiasm for religion, but it is quite as real, and certainly not less valuable. The state of mind of Kepler on discovering the laws of planetary motion was hardly less ecstatic than that of a religious visionary describing his sense of "spiritual" communion. Only in the case of the scientist, it is emotion guided by reason, not reason checked and partly throttled by emotion.

When, therefore, Matthew Arnold defined religion as morality touched with emotion, he substituted a fallacy for a definition. Primarily religion is as much a conviction as is the Copernican system of astronomy. It exists first as an idea; it only exists as an emotion at a later stage. There is really no such thing as a religious emotion, there are only emotions connected with religion. Originally all religion is in the nature of an inference from observed or experienced facts. This inference may not be of the elaborate kind that we associate with modern scientific work, but it is there. The inference is an illogical one, but under the conditions inevitable. And being an inference religion is not primarily an emotion but a conviction, and it must stand or fall by its intellectual trustworthiness. It seems, indeed, little less than a truism to say that unless men first of all *believed* something about religion they could never have emotions concerning it. Hope and fear may color our convictions, they may prevent the formation of correct opinions, but they originate in connection with a belief in every case. And an emotion, if it be a healthful one, must be ultimately capable of intellectual justification. When this cannot be done, when we have mere emotion pleaded as a ground for rejecting rational examination, we have irrationalism driven to its last ditch.

Chapter IV

The Argument from Existence

What, now, are the facts upon which the modern believer in deity professes to base his belief and what are the arguments used to defend the position taken up?

Premising that the reasons advanced for the belief in deity are more in the nature of excuses than aught else, we may take first of all the argument derived from the mere existence of the universe, with the alleged impossibility of conceiving it as self-existent. Along with that there may also be taken as a variant of the argument from existence, the alleged impossibility of a natural "order" that should result from the inherent properties of natural forces. Now it is at least plain that whatever difficulty there is in thinking of the universe as either self-existing or self-adjusting is in no degree lessened by assuming a God as the originator and sustainer of the whole. The most that it does is to move the difficulty back a step, and while with many "out of sight out of mind" is as true of their attitude towards mental problems as it is towards the more ordinary things of life, the policy can hardly be commended in serious intellectual discussions. It is not a bit easier to think of self-existence or self-direction in connection with a god than it is in connection with the universe. And if we must rest ultimately with an insoluble difficulty, it is surely better to stop with the existence we know rather than to introduce a second existence which for all we know may be quite mythical.

It is no reply to say that the idea of God involves self-existence. It does nothing of the kind, or at least it can do so only by our making yet another assumption that is as unjustifiable as the previous one. If God is a personality, we have no conception of a personality that is self-existent. The only personality that we know is the human personality, and that is certainly derived. Our whole knowledge of human personality is that of something which is derived from pre-existing personalities, each of which is a centre of derived influences. Of personality as either the cause or the commencement of a series we have not the slightest conception. And the man who says he has can never have carefully examined the contents of his own mind.

The truth is that the fact of the existence of the universe provides no ground for argument in favor of either Atheism or Theism. Existence is a common datum for all. Some existence must be assumed in all argument since all argument implies something that is to be discussed and explained. And for that very reason we can offer no explanation of existence itself, since all explanation means the merging of one class of facts in a larger class. The largest class of facts we have is that which is included in the term "universe," and we cannot explain that by assuming another existence—God—about which we know nothing. To explain the unknown by the known is an intelligible procedure. To explain the known by the unknown is to forsake all intellectual sanity. Thus every difficulty that surrounds the conception of the universe as an ultimate fact, surrounds the existence of God as an ultimate fact. You cannot get rid of a difficulty by giving it another name. And whether we call ultimate existence "God," or "matter," or "substance," is of no vital importance to anyone who keeps his mind on the real issue that has to be decided. If the question, What is the cause of existence? be a legitimate one, it applies no less to the existence of God than it does to the existence of matter, or force, or substance. All that we gain is another problem which we add to the problems we already possess. We increase our burden without enlarging our comprehension. If, on the other hand, it is said that we need an all embracing formula that will make our conception of the universe coherent, it may be replied that we have that in such a conception as the persistence of force. And it is surely better to keep to a formula that does at least work, than to devise one that is altogether useless.

The inherent weakness of the theistic conception will be best seen by taking an orthodox presentation of the argument under consideration. In his well-known work on "Theism," Professor Flint says "that granting all the atoms of matter to be eternal, grant that all the properties and forces, which with the smallest degree of plausibility can be claimed for them to be eternal and indestructible, and it is still beyond expression improbable that these atoms, with these forces, if unarranged, uncombined, unutilized by a presiding mind, would give rise to anything entitled to be called a universe. It is millions to one that they would never produce the simplest of the regular arrangements which we comprehend under the designation of course of nature." (*Theism*; pp. 107-8.)

Now this is an admirably clear and terse statement of an argument which is often presented in so verbose a manner that its real nature is, to a considerable extent, disguised. But in this case, clearness of statement makes for ease of refutation, as will be seen. For, instead of the statement being, as the writer seems to think, almost self-evidently true, it is almost obtrusively false. Instead of its being millions to one, given matter and force with all their present properties, against the present

41

arrangement of things occurring, it is inconceivable, assuming that nothing but the atoms and their properties exist, that any other arrangement than the present one should have resulted. For the present natural order is not something that is, so to speak, separable from our conception of natural forces, it is something that has grown out of and is the expression of the idea of nature. Thus, given a proper understanding of the principle of gravitation, and it is impossible to conceive an unsupported stone *not* falling to the ground. Given a proper conception of the properties of the constituents of a chemical compound, and we can only conceive one result as possible. In all cases our conception of what *must* occur follows from the nature of the forces themselves. This is necessarily the case since the conception of the ultimate properties of matter has been built up by the observation of the actual results. And one simply cannot conceive an alteration in these results without thinking of some alteration or modification of the causes of which they are the expression. What is true of the part is true of the whole. The present structure of the world stands as the inevitable outcome of the play of natural forces. This is both the expression of an actual fact and a condition of coherent thought. Uniformity of results from uniformity of conditions is a pre-requisite to sane thinking.

In reality, the expression "millions to one" is no more than an appeal to man's awe in facing a stupendous mechanism, and his feeling of impotence when dealing with so complex a subject as the evolution of a world. It can only mean that to a certain state of knowledge it *seems* millions to one against the present order resulting. But to a certain state of knowledge it would seem millions to one against so fluid a thing as water ever becoming solid. To others it is a commonplace thing and a necessary consequence of the properties of water itself. To a savage it would be millions to one against a cloud of "fire mist" ever becoming a world with a highly diversified fauna and flora. To a scientist there is nothing more in it than antecedent and consequent. Such expressions as its being "millions to one" against certain things happening is never really more than an appeal to ignorance; it means only that our knowledge is not great enough to permit our tracing the successive stages of the evolution before us. Once the scientific conception of the universe is grasped, the marvel is not that the present order exists, the marvel would be that any other "order" should be, or that any radical alteration in it should occur.

And there really is no need to throw the whole universe at the head of the skeptic. That is an attempt to overcome him with sheer weight. Intrinsically there is nothing more marvelous in the evolution of a habitable globe from the primitive nebula, than there is in the fact that an unsupported stone always falls to the ground. It is only our familiarity with the one experience and our lack of knowledge concerning the other that gives us the condition of wonder in the one case and lack of it in the other. In the light of modern knowledge "order" is, as W. H. Mallock says, "a physical platitude, not a divine paradox."

Moreover, if the odds are a million to one against the existence of the present arrangement existing, the odds would be equally great against the existence of any other arrangement. And as the odds are equally great against all—seeing that *some* arrangement must exist—there can be no logical value in using the argument against one arrangement in particular. The same question, "Why this arrangement and none other?" might arise in any case.

Finally, the absurdity of arguing that the "order" of nature compels a belief in deity may be seen by realizing the fact that our conception of order is itself the product of the experienced sequence which constitutes the order in question. Our ideas of order are not independent of the world, they are its product—

an expression of the relation between organism and environment. Given a different organism, with different sense organs, and the world would appear different. On the other hand the whole structure of man is the result of the existing conditions. Assume the order to be changed, and the human organism—presuming it still to exist, will undergo corresponding modifications. It would not find less order or less beauty, the order and the beauty would simply be found in another direction. And, presumably, the theist would still point to the existence of *that* order as clear proof of a designing intelligence.

Something needs to be said here on a more recent form of the argument from the "order" of nature than the one we have been discussing. There is no vital distinction between the old and the new form, but a variation in terms seems to produce on some minds a conviction of newness—itself a proof that the nature of the old form had never been fully realized.

This new form is that based upon what is called "Directivity." Recognizing that it is no longer possible to successfully dispute the scientific proposition that the state of the universe at any one moment must be taken as the result of all the conditions then prevailing, and, therefore, it is to the operation of the ultimate properties of matter, force, ether,—or whatever name we choose to give to the substance of the universe—it is argued that we nevertheless require some directing force which will set, and keep the universe on its present track.

But there is really nothing in this beyond the now familiar appeal to human impotence. "We do not know," "We cannot see," are quite excellent reasons for saying nothing at all, but the very worst ground on which to make positive statements, or on which to base positive beliefs. The only condition that would justify our making human ignorance a ground on which to make statements of the kind named would be that we had demonstrably exhausted the possibilities of natural forces, and no further developments were possible in this direction. Far from this being the case there is not a single man of science who would dissent from the statement that we are only upon the threshold of a knowledge of their possibilities.

And this assumption of "direction" is unconvincing, if not suicidal in character. Assuming that direction may have occurred, the fact of direction adds nothing to the qualities or possibilities of existence, any more than the "directivity" of a chemist adds to the possibilities of certain elements when he brings them into combination. Unless the possibilities of the compound were already in the elements guidance would be useless. And, in the same way, unless the capacity for producing the universe we see already existed in the atoms themselves, no amount of "direction" could have produced it. God simply takes the place of the chemist bringing certain chemical elements in, of the engineer guiding certain forces along a particular channel. But no new capacity is created, and all that is done by either the chemist or the engineer *might* occur without their interference. Otherwise it could not occur at all.

Now there is no denying that natural forces *do* produce the phenomena around us. That is undeniable. And whether there be a god or not this fact remains quite unaffected. All that God can do is to set up certain combinations. But this does not exclude the possibility of this combination taking place without the operation of deity. In fact, it implies it. Either, then, natural forces possess the capacity to produce the universe as we see it, or they do not. If they do not, then it is impossible for us to conceive in what way even deity could produce it. If, on the other hand, they have this capacity, the argument for the existence of deity loses its force, and the theist is bound to

45

admit that all that he claims as due to the action of deity might have happened without him. The theists own argument, if logically pursued ends in divesting it of all coercive value.

It is curious that the theist should fail to see that a much stronger argument for the operation of deity would have been of a negative character, to have proved that in some way God manifested an inhibitive influence and thus prevented certain things occurring which would have transpired but for his interference. Regularity, or "order" is, as we have seen, the necessary consequence of the persistence of force. And so long as natural forces continue to express themselves in the way in which experience has led us to expect there is no need for us to think of anything beyond. The principle of inertia is with us here, for if it be true that force will persist in a given direction unless deflected from its course by some other force, it must be equally true that *all* forces will work out a given consequence unless they are deflected from their course by the operation of some superior force.

Now if it were possible for the theist to show that in certain cases the normal consequences of known forces did not transpire, and that the aberration could not be accounted for by the operation of any other conceivable force, it might be argued with some degree of plausibility that there exists a controlling power beyond which answers to God. That might afford a plausible case for "directivity." But to insist upon the prevalence of "natural order" will not help the case for theism. It will rather embarrass it. It may, of course, impress all those whose conception of scientific method is poor—and sometimes one thinks that this is all that is deliberately aimed at—but it will not affect anyone else. To the informed mind it will appear that the Goddite is weakening his case with every step he takes in the direction of what he apparently believes to be a demonstration of its logical invulnerability.

Chapter V

The Argument from Causation

The argument from causation may logically follow that from existence, of which it may be regarded as a part. It is presented under various forms, and when stated in a persuasive manner, is next to the argument from design, probably as popular as any. The principal reason for this is, I think, that very few people are concerned with thinking out exactly what is meant by causation, and the proposition that every event must have a cause, wins a ready assent, and when followed by the assertion that therefore the universe must have had a cause, which is God, the reasoning, or rather the parody of reasoning, appeals to many. There is a show of reason and logic, but little more.

Quite unquestionably a great deals depends upon what is meant by causation, and still more upon the use made of the law of causation by theists. Thus we have seen it urged against Materialists that neural activity cannot be the equivalent of thought because they do not resemble each other. And in another direction we meet with the same idea in the assertion that the cause must be equal to the effect, by which it is apparently meant that the cause must be *similar* to the effect, and that unless we can discern in the cause the same qualities manifested by the effect, we have not established the fact of causation at all.

The complete and perfect answer to this last view is that the qualities manifest in an effect never are manifest in the cause, were it so it would be impossible to distinguish one from the other. The theist is, as is often the case, saying one thing and meaning another. What he says is that the cause must be adequate to the effect. There is no dispute here. But what he proceeds to argue is that the effect must be discernible in the cause, which is a different statement altogether. When he says that an effect cannot be greater than its cause, what he means is that an effect cannot be different from its cause, which is downright nonsense. He asks, How can that which has not life produce life? as though the question were on all fours with the necessity for a man to possess twenty shillings before he can give change for a sovereign.

Of course, the reply to all this is that the factors which when combined produce an effect always "give" something of which when uncombined they show no trace. There is no trace; of sweetness in the constituents of sugar of lead, or of blueness in the constituents of blue vitriol. In not a single case, if we are to follow the logic of the theist, is there a cause adequate to produce an effect, if we are to follow the reasoning of some theists; in each case we should have to assume some occult agent as responsible for the result. In reality and in strict scientific truth, it is of the very essence of causation that there shall be present in the effect some quality or qualities that are not present in the cause. And all the confusion may be eliminated if there is borne in mind the simple and single consideration that in studying an effect it is the qualities of a combination with which we are properly concerned. And to expect to find in analysis that which is the product of synthesis is in the highest degree absurd.

Sir Oliver Lodge in his little work on "Life and Matter" properly corrects the fallacy with which I have been dealing, and points out that "properties can be possessed by an aggregate or an assemblage of particles, which in the particles themselves did not in the slightest degree exist." But in his desire to find a basis for his theism immediately falls into an error in an opposite direction. We are on safe ground, he says, in asserting that "whatever is in a part must be in the whole." This is true if it is meant that as the whole contains the part, the part is in the whole. But in that sense the statement was hardly worth the making. What his argument demands is the meaning that as man is possessed of mind, and as man is part of nature, therefore nature, as a whole, manifests mind. And that is not true. Mind may be a special manifestation of a special arrangement of forces, and only occurring under special conditions. What Sir Oliver says, then, is that the properties of a part are in the whole, because the part is included in whole. What he implies, and without this implication his argument is meaningless, is that the properties of a part belong to all parts of the whole. And that is a statement so grotesquely untrue that I suspect Sir Oliver would be the first to disown the plain implications of his own argument.

And here is Sir Oliver's illustration of his argument:—

"the fact an apple has pips legitimizes the assertion that an apple tree has pips ... but it would be a childish misunderstanding to expect to find actual pips in the trunk of a tree."

Now, why should the fact that an apple has pips legitimize the statement that an apple tree has pips, any more than it legitimizes the statement that the soil from which it springs has pips? And if the tree has not actual pips, in what sense does it possess them? If the reply is that it possesses them potentially, one may meet that with the rejoinder that potentially pips, and everything else, including Sir Oliver Lodge, were contained in the primitive nebula. As a matter of fact the apple tree does not contain pips either actually or potentially. In his championship of theism our scientist forgets his science. What the apple tree possesses is the capacity for building up a fruit with pips *with the aid of material extracted from the soil beneath and from the air around*. These pips are no more in the tree than they are in the air or the soil—not even as a figure of speech. One might, from any point of view, as reasonably look for the color and shape and smell of an apple in the tree as to look for the pips. The properties of the tree is really one of the factors in the production of a result. Sir Oliver makes the mistake of writing as though the tree was the only factor in the problem.

This is not the place in which to enter on an exhaustive inquiry as to the nature of causation. It is enough to point out that the whole theistic fallacy rests here on the assumption that we are dealing with two things, when as a matter of fact we are dealing with only one. Cause and effect are not two separate things; they are the same thing viewed under two different aspects. When, for example, I ask for the cause of gunpowder and am told that it is sulfur, charcoal, and potassium nitrate, or for a cause of sulfuric acid and am given sulfide of iron and oxygen, it is clear that considered separately these ingredients are not causes at all. Whether charcoal and sulfur will become part of the cause of gunpowder or not will depend upon the presence of the third agent; whether sulfide of iron will rank as part of the cause of sulfuric acid will depend upon the presence of oxygen. In every case it is the assemblage of appropriate factors that constitute a real cause. But given the factors, gunpowder does not follow their assemblage, it is their assemblage that is expressed by the result. There is no succession in time, the result is instantaneous with the assemblage of the factors. The effect is the registration, so to speak, of the combination of the factors.

Now if what has been said be admitted as correct the argument for the existence of God as based upon the fact of causation breaks down completely. If cause and effect are the expressions of a relation, and if they are not two things, but only one, under two aspects, "cause" being the name for the related powers of the factors, and "effect" the name for their assemblage, to talk, as does the theist, of working back along the chain of causes until we reach God, is nonsense. Even if we could achieve this feat of regression, we could not reach by this means a God distinct from the universe. For, as discovering the cause of any effect means no more than analyzing an effect into its factors, the problem would ultimately be that of dealing with the question of how something already existing transformed itself into the existing universe. A form of a very doubtful Pantheism might be reached in this way, but not theism.

But here a fresh difficulty presents itself to the theist. A cause, as I have pointed out, must consist of at least two factors or two forces. This is absolutely indispensable. But assuming that we have got back to a point prior to the existence of the universe, we have on the theistic theory, not two factors, but only one. The essential condition for an act of causation is lacking. A single factor could only repeat itself. By this method the theist might reach "God." But having got there, there he would remain. He is left with God and nothing else, and with no possibility of reaching anything else.

We land in the same dilemma if we pursue another road. Philosophers of certain schools place existence in two categories. There is the world of appearance (phenomena), and there is the world of reality or substance (noumenon). We know phenomena and their laws, they say, but no more. We do not know, and cannot know, Substance in itself; and the theist

51

promptly adds that this unknown substance is but another name for God. The philosopher also warns us against applying the laws of the phenomenal world to noumena, reminding us that what we call "laws of nature" have been devised to explain the world as it presents itself to our consciousness. And to this we have the theological analogue in the warning not to measure the infinite by the finite or to judge God by human standards.

Now granting all this, let us see how the argument stands. The laws of phenomena belong exclusively to the phenomenal world. Their application and their validity are restricted to the world of phenomena. When we leave this region we are in a sphere to which they are quite inapplicable. What, then, can be meant by speaking of God as a "First Cause"? Cause is a phenomenal term, it expresses the relations between phenomena, and it has no meaning when applied to this assumed and unknown reality. We are in the position of one who is trying to use a color scale in a world where vision does not exist. The theist is trying, in a similar way, to use the conception of "cause," which is created to express the relations between phenomena, in a world where phenomena have no existence. Thus, when the theist, to use his own words, has traced back an effect to a cause, and this to a prior cause, and so on, till he has reached a "First Cause," what happens? Simply this. At the end of the chain of phenomena the theist makes a mighty jump and gains the noumenon. But between this and the phenomenon he can establish no relation whatever. It cannot be a cause of phenomena because on his own showing causation is a phenomenal thing. He has worked back along the chain of causation, discarding link after link on his journey. Finally, he reaches God and discards the lot. And here he is left clinging with *no intelligible way of getting back again.* If on the other hand, he relates God to phenomena he has failed to get what he requires. He has merely added one more link to his

52

chain of phenomena, and the "first cause" remains as far off as ever. For if God is not related to phenomena he ceases to be a cause of phenomena in the only sense in which he is of use to the theistic hypothesis.

Further, one may ask, Why travel back along the chain of causation to discover God? What is gained by travelling along an infinite series, and saying suddenly, "At this point I espy God." Confessedly we may trace back phenomena as far as we will without finding ourselves a step nearer a commencement. All we get is a transformation of pre-existing material into new forms. Consequently all the evidence that exists at the moment we cease our journey existed when we began it. In short, if God can be shown to be the efficient cause of phenomena anywhere, he can be shown to be the cause everywhere, and the proof may be produced through phenomena immediately at hand as well as from those removed from us by an indefinite number of stages. The evidence becomes neither stronger nor more relevant by being put farther back. Proof is not like wine, its quality does not improve with age. To say that we must pause somewhere may be true, but that is only reminding us that both human time and human energy are limited. But it is certainly foolish to first of all induce mental exhaustion, and then use it as the equivalent of a positive and valuable discovery.

And even though by some undiscovered method we had reached that metaphysical nightmare a cause of all phenomena, and in defiance of all intelligibility had christened it a "First Cause," how would that satisfy the "causal craving"? Professor Campbell Fraser very properly says that "the old form of each new phenomenon as much needs explanation as the new form itself did, and this need is certainly neither satisfied nor destroyed by referring one form of existence to another." If A. is explained by B. we are driven to explain B. by C., and so on indefinitely. Or if we can stop with A. or B. then the causal craving is not so persistent as was supposed, and man can rest content within the limit of recognized limitations. For what Professor Fraser calls an "absolutely originating cause" is only such so long as we have not reached it. We are satisfied with an imaginary B. as an explanation of the actual A. so long as B. does not come within our grasp. So soon as it has become the originating cause of the phenomenon in hand we are off on a further search. "First" has no other intelligible sense or meaning than this. "First" in relation to a given cluster of phenomenon we may grant; "First" in the sense of calling for no further explanation is downright theological lunacy.

An eternal "First cause" could only be such in relation to an eternal effect. And in that case it could not be *prior* to the effect since the effect is only the existing factors combined. Causation cannot carry us *beyond* phenomena since it has no meaning apart from phenomena. The notion that because every phenomenon has a cause therefore there must be a cause for phenomena as a whole—meaning by this for the sum total of phenomena—is wholly absurd. It is not sound science, it is not good philosophy, it is not even commonsense. It is simply nonsense which is given an air of dignity because it is clothed in philosophic language. You cannot rise from phenomena to the theist's God; first, because, as I have said, cause and effect are names for the relation that is seen to exist between one phenomenon and another, and the theist is seeking after something that is above all relations. To postulate something that is not phenomena as the cause of phenomena, is like discussing the possibility of a bird's flight and dismissing the possibility of an atmosphere. Secondly, causation can give no clue to a God because the search for causes is a search for the conditions under which phenomena occur. And when we have described these conditions we have fulfilled all the conditions required to establish an act of causation. The theist, in short,

54

commences with a wrong conception of causation. He proceeds by applying to one sphere language and principles from another, and to which they can have no possible application, and where they have no intelligibility. And having completely confused the issue, he ends with a conclusion which, even on his own showing, has no logical relation to the premises laid down.

Chapter VI

The Argument from Design

Kant called the argument from design "the oldest, the clearest, and the most adapted to the ordinary human reason," of all the arguments advanced on behalf of the belief in God. Kant's dictum, it will be observed, omits all opinion as to its quality, and his own criticism of it left it a sorry wreck. John Stuart Mill treated it far more respectfully, and commenced his examination of it with the flattering introduction, "We now at last reach an argument of a really scientific character," and, although he did not find the argument convincing, gave it a most respectful dismissal. The purpose of the present chapter is to show that the argument from design in nature is in the last degree unscientific, that the analogy it seeks to establish is a false one, that it is completely and hopelessly irrelevant to the point at issue, and that one might grant nearly all it asks for, and even then show that it does not prove what it sets out to prove. That such an argument should have, and for so long, exerted so much influence over the human mind, gives one anything but a flattering impression of the power of reason in human affairs.

True it is that of late years the argument from design has felt the influence of the growth of the idea of evolution, and the champions of theism have used it with much greater caution, and under an obvious sense that it no longer wielded its old authority. The fact that this is so forms a commentary on the statement so often made that man's craving for an ultimate cause leads to the belief in God. The truth being that man—the average man—only seeks for an explanation of immediate happenings. Once the immediate thing before him is explained his curiosity is allayed. The average man lives mentally from hand to mouth, and troubles as little about ultimate explanations as he does about the exhaustion of the coal supply.

It is a point of some significance that the perception of design in nature, as with the belief in deity, is, if one may use the expression, pre-scientific in point of origin. What I mean by that is that it originates at a time when no other explanation of the origin of natural adaptations existed. It did not establish itself as one of several rival explanations and in virtue of its own strength. It was established simply because no other explanation was at the time conceivable. And so soon as another explanation, such as that of natural selection, was placed before the world, the origin of adaptations as a product of an extra-natural designing intelligence became to most educated minds simply impossible. The perception of design in nature was, as a matter of fact, no more than a special illustration of the animistic frame of mind which reads vitality into all natural happenings. It is impossible to find in the statement that particular adaptations in nature are designed anything more scientific than one can find in the belief that rain is the product of a heavenly rain-cow, or that flashes of lightning are spears thrown by competing heavenly warriors. It is the language only that differs in the two cases. The frame of mind indicated in the two cases are identical.

The attractiveness of the argument from design lies in its

nearness to hand and in its appeal to facts, combined with the impossibility of verification. That nature is full of strange and curious examples of adaptation is clear to all, although the significance of these adaptations are by no means so clear. Moreover, a very casual study of these cases show that they are better calculated to dazzle than to convince. The presentation of a number of more or less elaborate facts of adaptation, followed with the remark that we are unable to see how such cases could have been brought about in the absence of a designing intelligence, is, at best, an appeal to human weakness and ignorance. The reverse of such a position is that if we had complete knowledge of the causes at work, the assumption of design might be found to be quite unnecessary. "We cannot see" is only the equivalent of we do not know, and that is a shockingly bad basis on which to build an argument.

When, therefore, an eminent electrician like Professor Fleming says, "We have overwhelming proof that in the manufacture of the infinite number of substances made in Nature's laboratory there must be at all stages some directivity," this can only mean that Professor Fleming cannot see the way in which these substances are made. It does not mean that he sees *how* they are made. And in saying this he is in no better position than was Kepler, who after describing the true laws of planetary motion, when he came to the question of *why* the planets should describe these motions fell back on the theory of "Angelic intelligences" as the cause. The true explanation came with the physics of Galileo and Newton, and with that, farewell to the angelic "directivity." The only reason for Kepler's angels was his ignorance of the causes of planetary motion. The only reason why Professor Fleming says that the atoms "have to be guided into certain positions to build up the complex molecules" is that he is unable to isolate this assumed directive force and to show it in operation; he is like a modern Kepler faced with something the cause of which he doesn't know, and lugging in "God" to save further trouble. It is an assumption of knowledge where no knowledge exists. "God" is always what Spinoza called it, the asylum of ignorance. When causes are unknown "God" is brought forward. When causes are known "God" retires into the background. "God" is not an explanation, it is a narcotic.

The argument from design rests upon the existence in nature of adaptations either general or special. And quite obviously the value of evidence derived from adaptations will be determined by the existence of non-adaptations. If, that is, it can be shown that a certain assemblage of forces produce adaptation, while in another instance they fail to produce it, it would then be logical to argue that the difference was due to the directive power being withdrawn in the latter case. But that as we know is never the case. What we see is always the same conditions producing the same effects. We are never able to say, "Here are natural forces working *minus* a directing intelligence, and here is an assemblage of the same forces working *plus* the addition of a directing intelligence." If we could do that we should be able to attribute the difference to the new factor. But this we are never able to do. And it is an elementary principle of scientific method that before we can assert the existence of a distinct force or factor, the possibility of isolation must be shown. Adaptation can, then, only be demonstrated by non-adaptation. And *non-adaptation in nature simply does not exist, except in relation to an ideal end created by ourselves.*

Surprising as this may appear to some, examination shows it to be no more than a truism, and that granted, the whole strength of the argument from adaptation, whether in the inorganic or the organic world, disappears.

To see the matter the more clearly, let us drop for a time the word "adaptation" and substitute the word "process." For that

59

after all is what nature presents us with. We see processes and we see results. It is because we create an *end* for these processes that we class them as well or ill adapted to achieve it. We make a gun, and say it is ill or well made as it shoots well or ill. But whether it carries straight or not the relation of the shooting to the construction of the gun remains the same. Judging the gun merely from its construction, the product answers completely to the combination of its parts. Constructed in one way the gun cannot but shoot straight. Constructed in another way the gun cannot but shoot crookedly. And the only reason we have for calling one good and the other bad is that *we* desire a particular result. But the goodness or badness has nothing to do with the thing itself. Its adaptation to the end produced is as perfect in the one case as in the other. It could produce no other result than the one that actually emerges without an alteration in the means employed. A thing is what it is because it is the combination of all the forces that produce it. And to ask us to marvel at the result of a process, when the one is the product of the other is like asking us to express our surprise that twice two equal four. Twice two equal four because four is the sum of the factors, and no one dreams of praising God because they don't sometimes make four and a half. The argument from adaptations in nature is, when examined, just about as impressive as the reasoning of the curate who saw the hand of Providence in the fact that death came at the end of life instead of in the middle of it.

Adaptation is not, then, a singular fact in nature, but a universal one. It is everywhere, in the case of death as in that of life. It is the same in the case of a child born a marvel of health and beauty as in that of one born deformed and diseased. There is nothing else but adaptations of means to ends in nature, however displeasing some of them may be to us. The "harmony" which the theist perceives in nature is not the expression of "plan," it is the inevitable outcome of the properties of existence. Given matter and force, and it requires no "directive intelligence" to produce the existing order, it would indeed require a God to prevent its occurrence.

It is the same if we take the case of animal life alone. To say that animal life is adapted to its environment, and to say that animal life exists, is to say the same thing in two ways. Whether animal forms are fashioned by "divine intelligence" or not, the fact of adaptation remains; for adaptation is the essential condition of existence. And as adaptation is the condition of existence, it follows that an animal's feelings, structure, and functions will be developed in accordance with the nature of the environment. If the conditions of existence were different from what they are animal life would show corresponding modifications. But all the same we should observe the same correspondence between animal life and its surroundings. Here, again, we have a fact transformed, without the slightest warranty, into a purpose.

Now, if the theist could prove that out of a number of equally possible lines of development living beings show one fixed form, and that against the compulsion of environmental forces, he would do something to prove the probability of some sort of guidance. But that we know cannot be done. The forms of life are infinite in number. They vary within all possible limits; and always in terms of environmental conditions. In brief, what is said to occur with God, can be shown to be inevitable without him. "God" in nature is a wholly gratuitous hypothesis.

Later it will be seen that the whole basis of the argument from design is fallacious; that it proceeds along altogether wrong lines, and that the final objection to it is that it is completely irrelevant to the point at issue. For the moment, however, we proceed with a criticism of the argument as usually stated.

It must be borne in mind that what the theist desires to reach is a *Creator*, but it is obvious that this plea can never give us more than a mere designer working on materials that already exist. Of necessity design implies two things, difficulties to be overcome, and skill or wisdom in overcoming them. Design is an understandable thing in connection with man, because man is always occupied in overcoming the resistance of forces that exist quite independently of him, and which operate without reference to his needs or desires. But it would be absurd to assume design on the part of one for whom difficulties had no existence, or on the part of one who himself created the forces that had to be overcome, and endowed them with all the properties which made the work of design necessary. Granting the relevance of the data upon which the belief in design rests, one could only assume, with Mill, that "the author of the Cosmos worked under limitations; that he was obliged to adapt himself to conditions independent of his will, and to attain his ends by such arrangements as these conditions admitted of."

In the next place, the argument for design is an argument from analogy, and an analogy can by its very nature never give a complete demonstration. It can never offer more than a probability, more or less convincing as the analogy is more of less complete. But in the case under consideration the analogy is considerably less rather than more. Paley's classical illustration—taken almost verbatim from Malebranche, but as old otherwise as the days of Greek philosophy, where a statute took its place—was that of a watch. And the conclusion was drawn that as the parts of a watch bear obvious marks of having been made with a view to a particular end, so the animal structure and the universe as a whole bear similar marks of having been designed. It is true that of late years the Paleyan form of the argument has been disavowed by most scholarly advocates of theism, but as they immediately proceed to make use of arguments that are substantially identical with it, the repudiation does not seem of great consequence. It reminds one of a government that is compelled by the force of public opinion to openly repudiate one of its officials, and having removed him from the office in which the misdemeanor was committed, immediately appoints him to one of an increased dignity and with a larger salary.

Thus, we have Professor Fiske saying that "Paley's simile of a watch is no longer applicable to such a world as this" ("Idea of God"; p. 131), and Prof. Sorley telling us that "the age of Paley and of the Bridgewater Treatises is past" (Moral Values and the Idea of God; p. 327), and Mr. Balfour repudiating Paley as having been ruled out of court by Darwinism ("Humanism and Theism," chapter II.). But as Fiske puts the flower in the place of the watch, Sorley, the moral nature of man, and Balfour, the conditions of animal life, it is not quite clear why if the Paleyan argument is invalid, the new form is any more intellectually respectable. The essence of the Paleyan argument was the assertion of a mind behind phenomena, the workings of which could be seen in the forms of animal life. And whether we find that proof in the growth of a flower, or in the moral sense of man, or in the creation of natural conditions that impel the development of life along a certain road, the distinction is not vital. We are still finding proofs of God in the structure of the world (where otherwise, indeed, are we to find it?) and we are still depending on the supposed likeness between the works of human intelligence and natural products.

And that analogy is wholly false. The argument from design aims at proving that *all* things are made by a creative intelligence. It is not merely animals that are designed; they are selected as no more than striking individual examples of a general truth. Everything, if theism be true, must be ultimately due to manufacture. But the whole significance of the Paleyan

63

argument from design is that behind the manufactured article which we recognize as such, there are other articles or other things that are not manufactured. The traveler, says Paley, who comes across a watch recognizes in the relation of its parts evidences of workmanship. But he does not see in the breaking of a wave on the shore, or in the piling up of sand in the desert, or in a pebble on the beach, the same tokens of workmanship. In the very act of attempting to prove that *some* things *are* made, the theist is compelled to assume that *all* things are not made. He can only gain a victory at the price of confessing a defeat.

But is there any real analogy between the works of man and the universe at large? Let us take a familiar example. It is, we are told in a very familiar illustration, as absurd to imagine that the world as it exists is the work of unguided natural forces, as it would be to believe that the rows of letters in a compositor's "stick" had of their own contained force arranged themselves in intelligible sentences. The absurdity of the last supposition is admitted, but why is that so? Obviously because we have the previous knowledge that the type itself is a manufactured thing, and that its arrangement in orderly sentences is the work of intelligent men. Thus, what occurs when we come across a particular example of type setting is that we compare our present experience with other experiences and recognize it as belonging to a particular class. So with the watch, the only reason we have for believing that a watch is made is that of our previous knowledge that such things are made. The present judgment is based upon past experience. But the case of animal forms, and still more the universe at large, offers no such analogy. We know nothing of world makers nor of animal makers. We have no previous experience to go upon, nor have we any things of a similar kind, known to be made, with which we can compare them. Instead of the points of resemblance between the two things being so numerous as to compel belief, they agree in one particular only, that of existence. At most all we are left with is the palpably absurd position that because man selects and adjusts means to a given end, therefore any combination of forces in nature which produce a certain result must also be the expression of conscious intention.

Some apparent force even to this flimsy conclusion might be given if nature could be said to be working towards a given end. But we do not find this. What we see is a multitude of forces at work, the action of each of which often results in the negation of the other. Put on one side the argument, but not the least pregnant fact that animal life is only maintained in the face of numerous agencies, inorganic and organic, that are apparently bent upon its destruction; put on one side also the fact that multitudes of parasites—as much the result of design as any other form of life—are constantly preying upon and destroying forms of life higher than themselves, and there still remain myriads of facts altogether inconsistent and completely irreconcilable with the hypothesis of a creative intelligence shaping the course of affairs to a given end. To take only one illustration of this. What is to be said of the myriads of animals that are born into the world only to perish before reaching an age at which they can play their part in the perpetuation of the species? Are we to believe that the same deity who fashioned these forms of life created at the same time a number of forces that were certain to destroy them? Clearly we are bound to assume, either that this hypothetical Being pursues a number of mutually destructive plans, or that there are a number of designers at work and at war with each other, or that none at all exist.

If we are to judge nature from the standpoint of human intelligence, then we must logically decide that it is full of waste, full of bungling, full of plans that come to nothing, of ends that are never realized, of pain and misery that might have been avoided by the exercise of almost ordinary intelligence. There are few animals concerning which a competent anatomist or physiologist could not suggest some improvement in their construction by which their functions might be more efficiently performed. Nor does it seem quite impossible to have so adjusted natural forces that the development of life might have been accomplished without the present enormous waste of material. It is almost stupid to ask, as did the late Dr. Martineau, what right have we to judge the world from "a purely humanistic point of view." The whole argument from design is based upon a humanistic point of view. The Atheist is only calling the attention of the theist to the consequences of his own argument.

I leave for a later chapter, the moral aspect of the design argument. I am at present concerned with its purely logical presentation. And the crowning charge here is not that it is inconclusive, not that it falls short, as Mill thought, of a complete analogy, the decisive rejection of it is based upon the fact that it is absolutely irrelevant. The argument has no bearing on the issue; the evidence has no relation to the case. What is the essence of the argument from design? It is based upon certain adaptations that are observed to exist. But adaptation is, as we have shown, a universal quality of existence. It exists in every case, and no more in one case than in another. And when the theist says that because certain things work together therefore god arranged it, an apt query is, How do you know? One may even say, Granting there is a God, how do you know that what is was actually designed by him? It is no use replying that the way things work together prove design, for things always work together. They cannot do otherwise. Any group of forces work together to produce a given result. That is part of the universal fact of adaptation which the theist holds up as though it were a divine miracle instead of, as Mallock says, a physical platitude.

Let us take an illustration from everyday life. A man tries his hand at building a bicycle. When it is finished the wheels are not true, the frame is unsteady, the whole thing is ready to fall to pieces and is absolutely un-rideable. Is any one warranted in declaring that because the parts have all been brought together by me therefore the resulting machine was an act of design? Clearly not. What I designed was a machine perfect after its kind. What appeared was the miserable structure that is before us. On the other hand that machine with all its imperfections might have been designed by me. I might, for some purpose deliberately have intended to make a machine that would not carry a rider. And when would anyone be logically justified in saying which of the two kinds of machines express my design? Clearly, only when he had a knowledge of my intention. Apart from a knowledge of an intention preceding an act the inference of design is unwarrantable.

Now, assuming the existence of a God, and who stands in the same relation to the world that I do to the machine, how can anyone know that the world as it is expresses design any more than did my home-made bicycle? In this case, as in the former, what is needed to justify the assumption of design is a knowledge of intention. One must know what the assumed maker intended and then see how far the actual result realizes it.

Design, in short, although it may be expressed in a physical form is not a physical thing, but a psychic fact. You cannot by examining physical processes and results reach design. You cannot start with a material fact and reach intention. You must begin with intention and compare it with the physical result. Things may be as they are whether design is involved or not. It is only by a knowledge of intention, and a comparison of that with the fact before us that we can be certain of design. Proof of design is not found in the capacity of certain clusters of circumstances or forces to realize a particular result, but in a knowledge that they correspond with an intention which we know to have existed before the result occurs.

To warrant a logical belief in design in nature three things are essential. First, one must assume that a God exists. Second, one must take it for granted that one has a knowledge of the intention in the mind of the deity before the alleged designed thing is brought into existence. Finally, one must be able to compare the result with the intention and demonstrate their agreement. But the impossibility of knowing the first two things is apparent. And without the first two the third is of no value whatever. For we have no means of reaching the first except through the third. And until we get to the first we cannot make use of the third. We are thus in a hopeless impasse. No examination of nature can lead back to God because we lack the necessary starting point. All the volumes that have been written, and all the sermons that have been preached depicting the wisdom of organic structures are so much waste of paper and breath. They prove nothing, and can prove nothing. They assume at the beginning all they require at the end. Their God is not something reached by way of inference, it is something assumed at the very outset.

What the theist does at every step of his reasoning is to read his own feelings and desires into nature. The design he talks so glibly about is in him, not outside of him. As well might a maggot in a cheese argue that the world was designed for him because the agreement between his structure and it are so harmonious. In relation to their surroundings man and the maggot are in the same position. And in the economy of nature man is of no more consequence than the maggot. There is a more complex synthesis of forces here than there, a more subtle exhibition of nature's infinite capacity for evolving fresh forms of life, and that is all. It is man himself who paints a distorted picture of himself on the surface of things, who reads his own passions and desires into nature, and then admires a marvel created by himself. To he who correctly visualizes the process of the evolution of deity, the existence of God is hardly to-day a question for discussion. There is a discussion only of the history of the belief, and in that is found its strongest condemnation.

Chapter VII

The Disharmonies of Nature

It has already been indicated that it is not really necessary, in order to prove design, to establish the fact that the design is perfect or that it exhibits complete goodness. It is enough that there be design. Its moral quality or value is quite another question. Nevertheless, it will be as well to deal with this latter aspect of the subject, and to see what kind of "plan" it is that nature does exhibit, even assuming the existence of some design.

Now it is evident that if there be design in nature, and if the design is the expression of a single supreme mind one quality of that plan should be unity. The products should, so to speak, dovetail into each other in such a way that they work together, and even harmonize with each other. But this is, notoriously, not the case. If from one point of view there is a certain harmony throughout the world of living beings in virtue of which life is preserved, it is at least equally true that from another point of view the harmony is one of destruction. And in the end death wins. Sooner or later death overtakes all forms of life, while in the grand total of living beings born into the world, a far larger number perish than can reach maturity. Wasted effort is the mildest judgment that can be passed upon these abortive attempts. And not only does death eventually win in the case of each individual, and against which may be set the consideration that in the economy of nature death plays a part in the development of life, but eventually death will, if we are to trust science, reap a sweeping and universal triumph by the consummation of terrestrial conditions that will render the maintenance of life impossible.

Or, again, the relations of species are clearly not what we have a right to expect in the working out of a reasonably wise and benevolent plan. It is a general truth that, with the exception of a few instances, chiefly connected with the relations existing between insects and flowers, the development of one species in relation to another is not that of mutual helpfulness. The general rule here is that of mutual injury. The carnivore prey on the herbivore and upon each other; and the herbivore crush each other by methods that are as effective as the method of direct attack. Any variation is "good" provided it be of advantage to its possessor. And the "good" of the one kind may mean the destruction of another order. All the exquisite design shown in the development of the finer feelings of man, and upon which theistic sentimentalists love to dwell, may be seen in the structure of those parasites which destroy man and bring his finer feelings to naught. The late Theodore Roosevelt says of the Brazilian forests:—

In these forests the multitude of insects that bite, sting, devour, and prey on other creatures, often with accompaniments of atrocious suffering, passes belief. The very pathetic myths of beneficent nature could not deceive even the least wise being if he once saw the iron cruelty of life in the tropics. Of course, "nature"—in common parlance a wholly inaccurate term, by the way, especially when used to express a single entity—is entirely ruthless, no less so as regards types than as regards individuals, and entirely indifferent to good or evil, and works

71

out her ends or no ends with utter disregard of pain and woe (Cited by E. D. Fawcett in *The World as Imagination*; pp. 571-2).

And Mr. Carveth Reade expresses the same thing in a more elaborate summing up:—

The merciless character of organic evolution appears to us, first, in reckless propagation and the consequent destruction. Every species is as prolific as it can be compatibly with the development of its individuals; and the deaths that ensue from inanition, disease, violence, present a stupefying scene. The best one can say for it is that, as life rises in the organic scale, the death rate declines. Yet even man still suffers outrageously by violence, disease, inanition; the notion that "Malthus's Law" no longer holds of civilized man is a foolish delusion. But more sinister than the direct destruction of life is the spectacle of innumerable species profiting by a life, parasitic or predatory, at the expense of others. The parasites refute the vulgar prejudice that evolution is by the measure of man, progressive; adaptation is indifferent to better or worse, except as to each species, that its offspring shall survive by atrophy and degradation. The predatory species flourish as if in derision of moral maxims; we see that though human morality is natural to man, it is far from expressing the whole of Nature. Animals, at first indistinguishable vegetables, devour them and enjoy a far richer life. Animals that eat other animals are nearly always superior not only in strength, grace and agility but in intelligence. There are exceptions to this rule; some snakes eat monkeys (thanking Providence), and the elephant is content with foliage; but compare cats and wolves with the ungulates that make a first concoction of herbs for their sake. It is true that our monkey kin are chiefly frugivorous; for it may be plausibly argued that man was first differentiated by becoming definitely carnivorous, a sociable hunter, as it were, a wolf-ape. Hence the advantage of longer legs, the use of weapons, the upright gait and defter hands to use and make weapons, more strategic brains, tribal organization, and hence liberation from the tropical forest, and citizenship of the world. The greater part of his subsequent history is equally unedifying: having made the world his prey, he says that God made the world to that end, and those who have preyed upon their fellows, and enslaved them, and flourished upon it, have declared that to have been the intention of nature. (*The Metaphysics of Nature*; pp. 344-5).

A perpetual pulling down and building up, and the building altogether dependent upon the demolition. The tiger built with tastes and capacities for catching the gazelle: the gazelle built with capacities that enable it to escape the tiger. There is no evidence here of the existence of a single mind working out an intelligent plan. At most we have either the proof for a number of warring powers, each one striving to destroy what the other is striving to create, or a single mind that has deliberately fashioned things so that each part may work for the destruction of the other part, the whole to presently end in a grand catastrophe.

But that is not all. If we limit our attention to man, can it be said that we find in the human structure what we might reasonably expect to find if man be indeed the crown of the divine plan, the event to which, for untold ages, all things were designedly tending? What we actually do find is that the structure of man, physically and mentally, is such as to altogether negative the notion of complete or harmonious adjustment to environment. That the human has within it a large number of vestigial structures—some scientists place it as high as one hundred and seventy—is now well known, and forms at the same time one of the evidences of evolution and an impeachment of the theistic theory. There is only need to instance now the vermiform appendage, which forms the seat of appendicitis, the "wisdom" teeth, of very little use, and one of the most fruitful of causes of disease of the teeth, the hair which covers the human body, now of no use whatever, except to form a lodgment for microbes, and so makes the acquisition of disease the more certain. In addition to the number of rudimentary organs that actually encourage disease—Metchnikoff counts among these the larger intestine—the body is full of rudimentary muscles and structures that when not positively harmful, impose a tax on the organism for which no corresponding service is performed.

The meaning and significance of these structures are, however, so well recognized that one need not dwell upon their existence. Not so well known is the complementary fact that just as in his physical structure man bears evidence of his emergence from lower forms of life, which result in a certain degree of disharmony between him and an ideal environment, so in his psychic life his instincts and feelings are often such as to prevent that ideal adaptation which so many desire. The earlier conception of optimistic evolutionists that the instincts of man were, through the operation of natural selection, converted into beneficent guides is quite faulty. In itself this was probably a survival of the theism which tried to prove that this was the best of all possible worlds, and which led evolutionists to try and prove that their theory was also ethically desirable. At any rate, the theory of the wholly beneficent nature of human instincts is not tenable. Our instincts are inherited from our animal ancestors; they were brought to fruition under conditions different in form from those which obtain with human beings, with the result that whether an instinct is helpful or the contrary depends largely upon the educational quality of the environment, and even then inherited tendencies may be so strong as to make them a source of danger to the community rather than of benefit.

It is noted, for example, that a deal of what may be called crime, or at least lawlessness, is the result of an individual being born with tendencies developed in a way that fits him for an environment of centuries ago, rather than an environment of to-day. Very many of our national heroes of a few centuries ago would rank as criminals to-day, just as many of our criminals to-day would, had they been born a few centuries since, have been handed down to us as examples of chivalry or of national heroism. Instead of what one may call the natural endowments of man pointing towards a more civilized form of life, they point to a less civilized form, while it is the artificially or socially induced feelings and ideas that point to a better future.

Thus, if we take the primitive or brute feeling of retaliation we find it assuming the form of war. And without discussing the value of war in the past, or even its admissibility in special circumstances in the present, I do not think it will be seriously disputed that the great need of the present is to transfer that feeling from the lower level of brute force to the higher one of adventure in the interests of science and human betterment. Here it is not the existence of a lofty "god-given" endowment that puts man out of harmony with his environment; it is, on the contrary, the operation of an earlier form of feeling manifestation which retards the coming of a better day.

There is, in fact, not a single quality of human nature that can be said to act with inerrancy. The baby seizes objects indiscriminately and puts them in its mouth. The man falling into the water does the very thing he should not do—throws up his arms. Intense cold lulls to somnolence, instead of rousing to activity. The love of children, on which the preservation of the human race depends, is absent with many; while with others the sexual instinct undergoes strange and morbid manifestations. A complete list of these disharmonies would fill a volume—indeed, Metchnikoff, in his "Nature of

Man," has filled half a volume with describing some of the instances of physiological disharmony, and then has not exhausted the list.

It would indeed seem as if nature, with its method of never creating a new organ or structure, but only transforming and utilizing an old one, had attached a penalty to every successful attempt to rise above a certain level. If man will walk upright she sees to it that his doing so shall involve a great liability to hernia. If he will live in cities, she has ready the ravage of consumption. If he will use clothing she makes him carry round a coating of useless hair as a method of trapping disease microbes. So soon as one disease is conquered another is discovered. Pleasures have their reverse side in pains, and to some pains the pleasures bear a small relation, being chiefly of the character of the pains being absent. As a social animal man is only imperfectly adapted to the state, there going on a constant warfare between his egoistic and altruistic impulses. In fact, it would certainly be an arguable proposition, if we allow intention in nature, to say that man was intended to remain at the animal level, and that, having so far defeated nature's intention, he is dogged by a disappointed creator, and made to pay the fullest price that can be exacted for every step of progress achieved.

Of course, of proof of design in nature there is positively none. Design, as I have said, is not a natural fact, but a purely human construction. But, if admitted, it is a two edged weapon. For, if assumed anywhere, it must be assumed to exist everywhere. And designing intelligence must be made responsible for the whole scheme. But this the most extravagant piety refuses to do. Either we have the primitive theory of a devil who divides with God the responsibility for the state of the world, or we have the plea that evil may be only good disguised, or good in the making, or it is argued that we have to contemplate the "plan" as a whole, and must wait for some future state to pass judgment. And whichever view we take, there is the implied admission that the plan of creation as we know it cannot be harmonized with the theory of God that modern theism places before us. And instead of man being the miracle of perfection that an earlier generation saw in his structure, we know that the human structure is such that, given the power to create, science could really fashion, in the light of its present knowledge, a better organism.

Finally, disharmony is implied in and necessitated by the very fact of progress. Progress means a better adjustment, and the discomfort of maladjustment is the spur to improvement. A perfect equilibrium is as impossible as perpetual motion, and it is only with a perfect equilibrium that change, which is the condition of progress, would cease. The ceaseless desire for something better is, therefore, in itself an impeachment of things as they are. It is an indication of there being something wanting, of the existence of a want of complete harmony between man and his surroundings. Nor is the case of the theist bettered if he retorts that without the sense of imperfection or of dissatisfaction there would be no such thing as a conscious striving after improvement. That may be admitted, but that is only proving that perfection can never be achieved, and that even in this last resort "God" has so designed things as to make a mock of man at the end. The want of complete harmony that is seen in the physical structure of man is carried over into his mental life. If theism be true man is mocked by a mirage. And the knowledge is made the more depressing by the belief that the plan is not accidental, it is not a product of the working of non-conscious forces, it is the preordained outcome of a plan that was deliberately resolved on by a being with full power to devise some thing wiser and better. At the side of that, any theory of things is, by comparison, hopeful and inspiring.

77

Chapter VIII

God and Evolution

There is no logical connection between what is called the "Moral government of the universe" and the belief in God, but it must be confessed that the criticism of the belief from the point of view of moral feeling is of considerable importance. This is in itself a striking illustration of the reaction of social developments on religious beliefs. For there is originally no connection between morality and the belief in God. Man does not believe in the gods because they are moral, but because they are there. If they are, to his mind, good, that is so much the better. But whether they are good or bad they have to be faced as facts. The gods, in short belong to the region of belief, while morality belongs to that of practice. It is in the nature of morality that it should be implicit in practice long before it is explicit in theory. Morality belongs to the group and is rooted in certain impulses that are a product of the essential conditions of group life. It is as reflection awakens that men are led to speculate upon the nature and origin of the moral feelings. Morality, whether in practice or in theory, is thus based upon what is. On the other hand, religion, whether it be true or false, is in the nature of a discovery. However crude or uninformed the thinking, the belief in God must be regarded as the product of reflection. The situation is not unfairly described by Dr. Jastrow:—

The various rites practiced by primitive society in order to ward off evils, or to secure the protection of dreaded powers or spirits, are based primarily on logical considerations. If a certain stone is regarded as sacred, it is probably because it is associated with some misfortune, or some unusual piece of good luck. Someone sitting on the stone may have died; or on sleeping on it may have seen a remarkable vision, which was followed by a signal victory over a dangerous foe.... In all this, however, ethical considerations are remarkable for their absence.... Taking again so common a belief among all peoples as the influence for good or evil exerted by the dead upon the living and the numerous practices to which it gives rise ... it will be difficult to discover in these beliefs the faintest suggestion of any ethical influence. It is not the good but the powerful spirits that are invoked; an appeal to them is not made by showing them examples of kindness, justice, or noble deeds, but by bribes, flatteries, and threats. (*The Study of Religion*; Ch. VI.).

So we have Tylor also endorsing this opinion by remarking that, "The popular idea that the moral government of the universe is an essential tenet of natural religion simply falls to the ground. Savage animism is almost devoid of that ethical element which, to the educated, modern mind, is the very mainspring of religion." And Hoffding says that, "In the lowest forms of it with which we are acquainted religion cannot be said to have any ethical significance. The gods appear as powers on which man is dependent, but not as patterns of conduct or administrators of an ethical world order.... Not till men have discovered ethical problems in practical life and have developed an ethical feeling ... can the figures of the gods assume an ethical character." ("Philosophy of Religion"; pp. 323-4).

It is quite unnecessary to multiply evidence, the truth of the matter would seem obvious. One cannot conceive man actually ascribing ethical qualities to his gods before he becomes sufficiently developed to formulate moral rules for his own guidance, and to create moral laws for his fellow man. The moralization of the gods will then follow as a matter of course. And thereafter we can plainly observe the operation of the moral sense on the belief in god, and upon the recognition of crude power. Man really modifies his gods in terms of the ideal human being. Paul's picture of a god who uses man as the potter uses his clay could never flourish in a society which believed in the "rights of man." And so soon as that conception develops so soon does man begin to revise his conception of god. So with almost every great change in the form of government or in the notions of right and wrong. In a slave state, God favors slavery. When slavery gives place to another form of labor the gods are equally vigorous in its condemnation. The history of the belief in witch burning, heresy hunting, eternal damnation, etc., all illustrate the same point—religious teachings are all modified and moralized in accordance with the changing moral conceptions of mankind. It is not the gods who moralize man; it is man who moralizes the gods.

The gods have their beginnings as mere powers. They are feared because they are, not for the moral value of what they are. Social development does all the rest. But with that development the feeling of helplessness, of weakness, decays and there arises the demand that if god is to be worshipped he must prove worthy of it. The conviction arises very gradually, but it is there, and it becomes a powerful solvent of religious ideas. Merely to govern is not enough, God must govern well, and in terms of what we have come to understand by the word "Justice." And to the minds of millions of moderns, when tried by that test the idea of god breaks down. That there is a god who rules the universe is one question; that he rules it well and in accord with what is understood when we talk of morality, is quite another. The two questions are quite distinct since the first might be true and the second false. We have already seen how slender are the grounds for believing in the first; we have now to show that the reasons for believing in the second are quite as unsatisfactory.

Theism has been defined as consisting in the belief in a God who is wise, powerful, and loving, and who has selected man as the object of his preferential care, and to this may be added the statement that most modern theists would extend that care to the whole of sentient life. "God's care" must be "over all his creatures," and although this care may be subservient to some wide and far-seeing plan, there must be nothing that looks like obvious carelessness or criminal neglect.

To what conclusion do the facts point when they are examined in the light of modern knowledge? Does the world supply us with the kind of picture that one would expect to see if it were really presided over by divine love under the guidance of divine wisdom, and backed by divine power? The proof that it does not is shown in the almost endless attempts made to harmonize the world as it is with the world as theory would have it be. And a theory that needs so much defending, explaining, and qualifying must have something radically weak about it. That there is evil in the world all admit, that it offers *prima facie* objection to the theistic hypothesis is confessed by the many attempts made to fit in this evil with the existence of God, to prove that it works in some mysterious way for some larger good, or that its presence cannot be dispensed with profitably. The question of why the world is as it is with a god such as we are told exists, is, as Canon Green says, "the really vital question, for it touches the very heart of religion." ("The Problem of Evil"; p. 46.) How, then, does the Theist deal with it?

Broadly, two methods are adopted. In the one case we are presented with the order of the world, or the course of evolution, as indicative of a beneficent scheme. This claims to freely adopt all that science has to say concerning the development of life and to prove that this is in harmony with the legitimate demands of the moral sense. The second is the more orthodox way, and taking the world as it is, claims that pain and suffering play a disciplinary and educational part in the life of the individual. We will take these in the order named.

When dealing with the argument from design little was said concerning the evolutionary explanation of the special adaptations that meet us in the animal world. It was thought better to fix attention on the purely logical value of the argument presented. It is now necessary to look a little closer at the ethical implications of the evolutionary process.

It has been pointed out that all life involves a special degree of adaptation between an organism and its environment. Destroy that adjustment and life ceases to exist. How is that adjustment secured? The answer of the pre-Darwinian was that it represented a deliberate design on the part of God. Against this Darwinism propounds a theory of automatic or mechanical adjustment which makes the calling in of deity altogether gratuitous. And it remains gratuitous, no matter how far the scope of the theory of natural selection may be modified. But given the continuous variations which we know to exist with all kinds of life, given any sort of competition between animals as to which shall live, given even a degree of adaptation below

82

which an animal cannot fall and live, and it is at once plain that the better adaptations will live and the poorer adapted will be eliminated. This process is analogous to that by which man has managed to breed so many varieties of domesticated animals and plants, some of the varieties presenting so marked a difference from the original type that if found in a state of nature they would often be classed as a distinct species. Man *selects* the variation that pleases him, eliminates or segregates the type that does not, and by following up the process eventually produces a distinct and fixed variation. It was because of the likeness of what goes on in the case of the breeder to what we see actually going on in nature that Darwin used the phrase "Natural Selection" as descriptive of the process. It was not an exact phrase, and it was not meant to be exact. For one thing—a very important thing, while a breeder selects, nature eliminates. Man's action, in relation to the type preserved, is positive. Nature's attitude in relation to the type preserved is negative. This is a very important distinction; and it is one that is fatal to the claims of theism. For if it points to a plan in nature it points to one that aims at killing off all that can be killed, and only sparing those who are able to protect themselves against its attack. And one is left wondering at the type of mind which can see goodness and wisdom in a plan that goes, on generation, after generation manufacturing an inferior or defective type in enormous numbers in order that a few superior specimens may be found, these in their turn to become inferior by the arrival of some other specimens a little more fortunate in their endowment. One hardly knows at which to marvel the most—at the clumsiness of the plan, or at the brutality of the design.

It was soon realized that the old argument from design was no longer possible. But if one can only get far enough away from the possibility of proof or disproof there is always a chance for the Goddite. So it was argued that inasmuch as natural selection meant the emergence of a "higher" type, and as there was no room for design within the process, might not the process itself be an expression of design? There might still be room for what Huxley, with one of those foolish concessions to established opinion which is the bane of English thought, called the "wider teleology." This was a teleology which placed a designing mind at the back of the evolutionary process, and arranging it with a view to a preconceived end. The process then becomes, to use Spencer's phrase, a "beneficent" one, since it eliminates the poorer specimens and leaves the better ones to perpetuate the species. We are thus asked to imagine a divine wisdom selecting the better and destroying the inferior much as an omniscient Eugenicist might destroy at birth all human beings of an undesirable type.

The weakness of the thesis lies primarily in the fact that in the case of the breeder he has to take the animal as he finds it, subject to the play of forces, the characteristics of which are determined for him. He has to make the best of the situation. In the case of the deity he creates the animals with which he is assumed to be experimenting, he creates the forces with all their qualities, and thus determines the nature of the situation. Quite certainly no breeder would waste his time in breeding over a number of generations if he could secure the desired type at once. The whole of the argument of the advocate of the wider teleology is that God wanted the higher type. But if that is so why did he not produce it at once? What useful purpose could be served by producing at the end of a lengthy and murderous process what might just as well have been secured at the beginning? It is not wisdom but unadulterated stupidity to take thousands of years securing what might have been as well done in the twinkling of an eye.

There is, in short, no justification in the creation of a process so long as the end at which the process is aiming can be reached by a less tortuous method. As Mr. F. C. S. Schiller says:—

So long as we are dealing with finite factors, the function of pain and the nature of evil can be more or less understood, but as soon as it is supposed to display the working of an infinite power everything becomes wholly unintelligible. We can no longer console ourselves with the hope that "good becomes the final goal of ill," we can no longer fancy that imperfection serves any secondary purpose in the economy of the universe. A process by which evil *becomes* good is unintelligible as the action of a truly infinite power which can attain its end without a process; it is absurd to ascribe imperfection as a secondary result to a power which can attain all its aims *without* evil. Hence the world process, and the intelligent purpose we fancy we detect in it must be illusory.... God can have no purpose, and the world cannot be in process.... If the world is the product of an infinite power it is utterly unknowable, because its process and its nature would be alike unnecessary and unaccountable. (*Riddles of the Sphinx*; pp. 318-19).

Besides, as I have already pointed out, in the process as it meets us in nature there is not a selection for preservation, but a selection for killing. With the breeder preservation is primary. It is of no value to him to kill, it is the preservation of a desired type that is all important. In nature, so far as we can see, the whole aim is to destroy. It is not the fittest that are preserved so much as it is the unfitest that are killed. The fittest are left alive for no other apparent reason than that nature is unable to kill them. The truth of this is seen in the fact that where there is no death there is no evolution of a "higher" type. In the case of diseases that kill there is a gradual development of an immune type—which introduces the paradox that the healthiest diseases from which a race may suffer are those that are most deadly. Where a disease does not kill there is no development against it. It is the winnowing fan of death that makes for the

85

development of animal life. And the correct picture of nature—
if we must picture an intelligence behind it—would be that of
an intelligence aiming at killing all, and only failing in its
purpose because the natural endowment of some placed them
beyond its power.

And, without examining the question begging word "higher," it
may be said that natural selection does not make for the
uniform covering of the earth with representatives of higher
types. If in some parts of the world the higher have replaced
the lower types, elsewhere the lower have replaced the higher.
Natural selection, in fact, works without reference to whether
the form which survives is "higher" or "lower." All that matters
is adaptation. The germ of malaria renders whole tracts of the
earth uninhabitable to those whom we consider representative
of the higher culture. In other parts an alteration of the rainfall
may crush out a civilization, and leave a handful of nomadic
tribes as the sole denizens of lands where once a lofty
civilization flourished. Throughout the whole of nature there is
never the slightest indication that forces operate with the
slightest reference to what we are accustomed to consider the
higher interests of the race.

Moreover, from the standpoint of an apologetic theism, we are
entitled to ask precisely what is meant by this justification of
the evolutionary process in terms of the production of a higher
type. The justification of a painful or a costly experience by an
individual is two-fold. First, it is the only way, perhaps, in
which certain things may be learned or accomplished, and,
second, it is the individual who passes through the experience
who benefits thereby. But suppose a person entered on a
course of training with the absolute certainty that he would
never survive it. Should we be justified in forcing the course on
him? Clearly not. The whole would be regarded as a wasted
effort and as an exhibition of gratuitous cruelty.

86

Now when we look closely at this evolutionary process, who is it that benefits thereby? In a vague way we speak of the human race benefiting. But the human race is made up of individuals, and while it may be said the individual benefits from the experience through which the human race has passed, it cannot be truthfully said that he is the better because he has gained from experience. He does not pass through the discipline, he simply registers, so to speak, the result. And, therefore, so far as he is concerned, he is exactly in the position that the first man would have been had he possessed the endowment, social, and individual, which the present man has. There is no greater fallacy than that contained in the common saying that man learns through experience. Individually, so far as civilization is concerned, that is not true. Were it true, civilization would be impossible. If each man had to start where our primitive ancestors started, and learn from experience, we should end where the first generation of socialized human beings ended, and the generations of men would represent an endless series of first steps to which there would be no second ones. What the individual learns from experience is very little and would never serve to lift him from out the ranks of savagery. What he learns from the experience of the human race is much, and gives the whole distinction between the civilized man and the savage. It is the discipline of the race, that experience which meets each of us in the form of traditions, counsels, institutions, etc., from which we get the really vital lessons of life. But if that is so the attempted justification of natural processes on the ground that God designed them as they are so that man might learn from experience breaks down. The individual does not so learn, but is presented with the products of the experience of others, and which he accepts in the vast majority of cases without even putting it to the test. And, therefore, the method by which man learns was open from the start. Had there been some *man* who could have told us generations ago all that has been slowly discovered since, we should all have been the better for it, and we should have learned then exactly as we have learned since. And if God was really anxious to teach us, what possible objection could there be to his teaching us in some such way? In other words, how can we justify the process if the result is possible by any other method?

The standpoint of the theist is that God develops the species in order to benefit the individual. But the order is that the individual is sacrificed to benefit the species—so far as any benefit can be traced. For it must be noted that it is not the individual who has passed through all the suffering, who has lived through the years of semi-animal life, or through the years of tyranny, that finally emerges strengthened and triumphant. It is a different individual altogether. The greatest benefit is secured by those who come latest, and who have done the least to secure it. The reward bears no relation to the personal desert. And at the end what happens? If we are to be guided by the lessons of science, we must believe that one day the human race will cease to exist, just as certainly as one day it began to exist. And what are we to think of the almighty wisdom and goodness which is responsible for all? An almighty intelligence designs a process to produce a perfect animal through the sufferings of myriads of other animals. It takes thousands and thousands of generations to complete the process, and meantime every year is bringing the whole plan nearer to extinction. Divine wisdom! Anything nearer complete stupidity and futility it would be difficult to conceive.

I know that at this point it will be said that I am leaving out of account the future life, and that the story of human growth is to be continued elsewhere. But that will certainly not meet all that has been said above. And it is a curious manner of meeting an objection based upon the only phase of existence that we know with assurance to tell us that our indictment will receive a complete refutation in another state of existence of which we know nothing at all. The reply is in itself an admission of the truth of the charges. If life admitted of a moral justification here there would be no need to appeal to some other life in which these blemishes are made good. If some other life is needed to correct the moral abnormalities of this one, then the indictment of the Atheist is justified. And one is left again wondering why, if almighty intelligence could make all things straight in the next world, why the same intelligence could not have made the necessary corrections in this one.

The truth is that the God of the evolutionary process is as much a myth as is the god of special creation. He has all the blemishes of the other one—one step removed. The Paleyan God had at least the merit of coming to close grips with his work. The evolutionary one shields himself behind the fact that the work is done by his agents, and then it is found that he created the agents for this special work and all that they do is the product of the qualities with which he endowed them. If anything the evolutionary deity is more objectionable than the older one. And if theists will examine nature candidly and with an open mind, they will see that it is so. I do not know that anyone has drawn a more truthful picture of natural processes as they appear from the point of view of being the product of a divine intelligence than has Mr. W. H. Mallock, and his picture is the more deadly as coming from a champion of theism. If, he says, theists will look the facts of the universe steadily in the face:

What they will see will astonish them. They will see that if there is anything at the back of this vast process, with a consciousness and a purpose in any way resembling our own— a being who knows what he wants and is doing his best to get it—he is instead of a holy and all-wise God, a scatter-brained, semi-powerful, semi-impotent monster. They will recognize as clearly as they ever did the old familiar facts which seemed to them evidences of God's wisdom, love, and goodness; but they will find that these facts, when taken in connection with the others, only supply us with a standard in the nature of this Being himself by which most of his acts are exhibited to us as those of a criminal madman. If he had been blind, he had not sin; but if we maintain that he can see, then his sin remains. Habitually a bungler as he is, and callous when not actively cruel, we are forced to regard him, when he seems to exhibit benevolence, as not divinely benevolent, but merely weak and capricious, like a boy who fondles a kitten and the next moment sets a dog at it, and not only does his moral character fall from him bit by bit but his dignity disappears also. The orderly processes of the stars and the larger phenomena of nature are suggestive of nothing so much as a wearisome Court ceremonial surrounding a king who is unable to understand or to break away from it; whilst the thunder and whirlwind, which have from time immemorial been accepted as special revelations of his awful power and majesty, suggest, if they suggest anything of a personal character at all, merely some blackguardly larrikin kicking his heels in the clouds, not perhaps bent on mischief, but indifferent to the fact that he is causing it....

The truth is, if we consider the universe as a whole, it fails to suggest a conscious and purposive God at all; and it fails to do so not because the processes of evolution as such preclude the idea that a God might have made use of them for a definite purpose, but because when we come to consider these processes in detail, and view them in the light of the only purposes they suggest, we find them to be such that a God who could deliberately have been guilty of them would be a God too absurd, too monstrous, too mad to be credible. (*Religion as a Credible Doctrine*; pp. 176-8).

As we have already seen, the attempt to find a plan in the processes of evolution breaks down hopelessly. On analysis, the supposed plan turns out to be nothing more than a perception of some sort of regularity, and as regularity is an inescapable condition of existence, all that it proves *is* existence. On that point there is no dispute. And the moral justification of the cosmic process while intellectually indefensible, adds an element of moral repulsion. That the process as we know it is morally repugnant is shown by the appeal to the future, the request to suspend judgment till such time as the plan is completed, when it is hoped that the end will justify the means. God, it is trusted, will justify himself in the future. But in his anxiety to impress upon us the fact that God has a moral future the theist forgets that he has had a past, and that past is a black one. The uncounted generations of suffering in the past is not to be compensated by a probable happiness in the future. The myriads of organisms that have lived incomplete lives, and ended them in deaths of suffering are not cancelled by the probability that at some time, still in the future, a comparatively small number will lead lives of happiness. The record is there, "there is blood upon the hand," and not all the apologies of a self-convicted animism can ever wipe it clean.

Chapter IX

The Problem of Pain

The problem of how to harmonize the existence of a God as believers picture him to be with a world such as experience discloses, is as old as theology. And the problem will disappear only when theology is given up as an aggregate of question begging words and gratuitous hypotheses based upon a foundation of primitive ignorance and inherited delusion. For the majority of those questions that are properly called theological are not of the necessary order. Questions such as those connected with the mutations of matter, the development of life, the growth of society, or the nature and clash of human passions cannot be evaded. They are present in the facts themselves. But the problems of theology are self-created; they arise out of certain beliefs, and have no existence apart from those beliefs. They are the joint product of beliefs which are wholly useless, in conflict with facts with which they cannot be squared.

What is known as "The Problem of Evil" is an apt illustration of the truth of what has been said. Here there is created a problem which is not alone quite gratuitous, but it succeeds in inverting the real question at issue. For unless we accept the world as the product of a good and wise God, there is no problem of evil for us to explain. The problem of evil is, given such a deity, how to account for the existence of evil, or, if it exists, how account for its continuance. The problem is created by the theory. Dismiss the theory and no problem is left. And it is in line with what is done in other directions, that, having created the difficulty, the theist should present it to the non-theist as one of the questions that he must answer.

In reality there is no problem of evil in connection with ethics. The ethical problem is not the existence of evil, but the emergence of good; not, that is, why do men do wrong, but why do they do right. That life should cease to be is not at all wonderful, but that with so many potential dangers around the organism, the actions of living beings should become so automatically adapted to their surroundings as to shun the actions which destroy life, and perform such actions as maintain it—at least, to such an extent as secures the preservation of the species—may well arouse surprise and give birth to enquiry. So with the question of evil and suffering in the world. That these exist is undeniable, but the enquiry they suggest is only on all fours with the enquiry suggested by any other natural fact, while the ethical problem centers, not around the existence of wrong action, but around the emergence of right conduct. It is the evolution of happiness that forms the kernel of the ethical problem, not the evolution of pain.

The earlier form of the Christian apologetic took the form of a dualistic theory of the world. There were two powers, God and the devil, and between them they shared the responsibility for all good and evil. So far, good. But this was clearly saving the goodness of God at the expense of his omnipotence. Moreover, if God was to be thought of as the creator of the universe, the theory, as Mill said, paid him the doubtful compliment of making him the creator of Satan, and, therefore, the creator of evil once removed. Or, if not, God and the devil were left as rival monarchs quarrelling over a territory that appeared to exist apart from and independent of either.

But nowadays the devil has gone out of fashion. Very few of the clergy ever mention him, and although an attempt was made to reinstate him some years ago by the author of "Evil and Evolution," the endeavor was a failure. And bereft of the convenient scapegoat, the devil, the present day theist is compelled to attempt an apology for evil that will appeal to natural and verifiable facts for confirmation, or which must, at least, not be in conflict with them. If theism is to stand, a place and a meaning must be found for the evil in the world, and found in such a way that it either relieves God of the responsibility for its existence or its being can be shown to harmonize with his assumed character. It is no longer possible to fall back on Paul's position that the potter is at liberty to doom one pot to honor and the other to dishonor. The moral responsibility for the kind of pots he turns out cannot be so easily evaded. As Professor Sorley says, "If ethical theism is to stand, the evil in the world cannot be referred to God in the same way as the good is referred to him." Somehow, he must be relieved of the responsibility for its existence, or a purpose for it must be found.

Now, curiously enough, modern theists hover between the two positions. Professor Sorley, representing one position, says that the only way to avoid referring evil to God is by "the postulate of human freedom." ("Moral Values and the Idea of God," p. 469.) This is also the way out adopted by Canon Green in "The Problem of Evil," and it turns upon a mere play on words. Thus, Canon Green says that there is one thing God could not do. "He could not force him to be good, i.e., to choose virtue freely, for the idea of forcing a free being to choose involves a contradiction." And Professor Sorley says more elaborately that

94

"things occur in the universe which are not due to God's will, although they must have happened with his permission ... a higher range of power and perfection is shown in the creation of free beings than in the creation of beings whose every thought and action are pre-determined by their Creator," and while he admits there is limitations to man's power of choice, he holds that there is one form of choice that is always there, and that is the choice of good and evil. ("Moral Values and the Idea of God," pp. 469-70.)

In all this one can see little more than verbal confusion. To commence with Canon Green, which will also cover much that Prof. Sorley says on the same point. When we are told man must choose virtue freely in order that what he does shall partake of the character of morality, it is plain that he is using the word "forced" in two senses. In the one sense force may mean no more than a determinant. Thus we may say that our sympathies *force* us to act in such and such a way. Or the religious man may say that the love of God forces him to act in such and such a manner. Force here means any consideration that will lead to action, and no one can object to its use in this sense.

A second meaning of force is that of compulsion from without, as when a strong man gets hold of a weak one and by exertion of physical strength compels him to do something that he is disinclined to do, or when one forces another by threat of punishment. In this latter sense no one dreams of harmonizing force with moral action. Neither law nor common sense does so. But compulsion in the sense of one's actions being forced by a mental or moral disposition no one outside an asylum would dispute. And what Canon Green does is to ask us to reject the idea of a moral action being forced, in the sense of external compulsion, and then uses it in the sense of an absence of dispositions that will lead to certain courses of conduct.

It is probable that the Canon would reject this interpretation of his statement, but if it does not mean this, then his argument is unintelligible. For if it is admitted that what man does is the product of his mental or moral dispositions, in other words, of his nature, and if, as is undeniable, the nature with which he fronts the world is the product of heredity and environment, he would no more be "forced" to do good had God given him impulses strong enough to overcome all tendency to evil than he is now when his impulses come to him from his ancestors and his general social heredity.

All that is implied in a moral act is free choice. But choice is free, not when it is independent of organic promptings; that is absurd; but when those organic promptings are allowed to find expression. There is no other rational meaning to "choice" than this. Choice does not tell us how it is determined, on that point it can say nothing, any more than a child can say why it chooses sugar in preference to cayenne pepper. Its choice, we say, is determined by its taste. And its taste is determined by — ? To answer that question we must call in the chemist and the physiologist, and they probably will tell us why our choice moves in one direction rather than in another.

When men like Canon Green talk of the morality of an action being dependent upon our *choice* between right and wrong, what they probably have in their minds is the perception of right and wrong. For we may perceive the possibility of one course while we are performing another. But the power of choice is clearly limited. A man cannot choose to be a mathematician, however much he may see the desirability of becoming one. And many a man may in the moral sphere see the advisability of his being different in character from what he is, but may altogether lack the capacity of becoming such. And the power of choice differs not only with each individual, but with the same individual at different times. Finally, the more fixed the character of the individual the less conscious he is of choice, or of a sense of freedom to do differently from what he actually does, and as this applies with equal force to character, whether it be good or bad, we reach, finally, the suicidal position that the more fundamentally moral a man becomes, the less moral he is.[5]

Now seeing that all our educational processes aim at making the good character, so to speak, automatic, that is, to quite fill the mind with worthy motives and wise power of choice, and seeing also that a character is good so far as this is done, will some one explain in what way moral character would have suffered had God so made man that he would have had intelligence enough to always choose the good and reject the bad? For, be it noted, the apology put forward for the present state of affairs is that man is in a state of probation, he is passing through a course of moral discipline, and it is essential that he should experience the possibility to do wrong, and even to occasionally do the wrong. And the end of the process of tuition is, what? The production of a perfect being in whom there shall not be a proneness to do wrong, to whose purified moral nature wrong doing shall be quite foreign. That is to say that we are to reach as a result of this long roundabout process, with all its waste and bungling, just what might have been established at the beginning. For either the perfect moral being is without the quality which we have just been assured is essential to morality, or the whole argument is reduced to nonsense.

For it is impossible to assume that the bad man chooses to be bad with a full perception of the consequences of his actions, and at the same time with the power to do otherwise. We all

---

[5] I have discussed this question at length in my "Determinism or Free Will."

agree that the *right* choice is ultimately a *wise* choice, and that if we could all trace out the consequences of all we do, we should realize that it was to our real interest to act rightly. And if that is admitted, it follows that the "choice" to do evil is the product of short-sightedness, or of some defect of temperament which prevents our standing up against the temptations of the moment. And our ethical education is mainly directed to making good this defect in our make up. But suppose that amount of wisdom or strength had been an endowment of our nature from the outset, is there any conceivable way in which we should have been the worse for it? For even as it is there are some people who do make a fairly wise and right choice, and whose high-water mark of excellence is not reached through the crime and folly of the revival meeting convert. Are they the worse because they have never yielded to evil? Is the naturally good man really a less worthy character than the one whose comparative goodness is only reached through and after a lengthy course of evil living? And if not, in what way would the human race have been worsened had we all been as fortunately circumstanced? If it was really God's purpose to have a race of men and women who should be both good and wise, it remains for the theist to show in what way the plan would not have been as well served by making them at once with a sufficiency of intelligence to act in the real interests of themselves and of all around them.

Coming closer to earth the theist attempts to find a justification for the existing order of things by finding a use for pain and suffering in their educational influence on human nature, and in the impossibility of altering for the better the consequences of natural law.

The real question at issue, says one of the most eloquent of modern theists, the late Dr. Martineau, is "whether the laws of which complaint is made work such harm that they ought

98

never to have been enacted; or whether, in spite of occasional disasters in their path, the sentient existence of which they are the conditions has in its history a vast excess of blessing." (Study of Religion II., p. 91.) And Canon Green, who uses some of Dr. Martineau's ideas without the latter's eloquence or power of reasoning, asks, "If God were to say, 'You condemn me for this suffering! Well, take my creative power and re-create the world to please yourself and to suit your own sense of justice and mercy'" could we think out a world that should be better than this one? (Problem of Evil, p. 48.)

Now both these methods of raising the question—and they are representative of a whole group—serve but to confuse the issue. For no one denies that some benefit may result from the present cosmical structure. But that does not touch the complaint that the structure is not such as fits in with the existence of a presiding intelligence such as theism asks us to accept. And the question of Canon Green's whether we could turn out a better universe than the one that actually exists, is wide of the mark also. If I purchase a motor car as the work of a genius in car-building, and find when I get my purchase home that it cannot be made to run, it does not destroy the justice of my complaint to ask whether I could build a better one or not. The important thing is that the car is not what it should be, and judging by the product the builder is not what he is represented to be either. Dr. Martineau was far too keen a controversialist to adopt Canon Green's foolish retort, but he does seek to parry the force of the atheist criticism by saying that God "if once he commits his will to any determinate method, and for the realization of his ends selects and institutes a scheme of instrumental rules, he thereby shuts the door on a thousand things that might have been done before." (*Study*, p. 85). To that one may reply, so much the worse for his judgment; while if the fact of his having once adopted a "determinate method" caused him to resolve to stick to it, in spite of its consequences in practice, and irrespective of the beneficial results that might have followed its modification, we can only regret that the deity was not acquainted with Emerson's opinion that "a foolish consistency is the bugbear of little minds." Even what is said to be the greatest mind of all might easily have benefited from the warning.

Canon Green tries another line of reply, which is not in the least more convincing. He pictures to us a father who, by misappropriating trust funds, brings disgrace to the whole of his family. The mother is driven to despair and drink. The sister dies for want of food, the brother finds his career ruined. The disaster is complete, and Canon Green says it is inevitable because we cannot have a world in which the relations of parents and children exist without having them suffer from each other's faults. So far as the present world goes that is true. But it is certainly a strange reply to the complaint that an arrangement is unjust to say that as the injustice results from the arrangement, therefore, we have no cause for complaint. And that *we* are unable to make a better world is beside the mark. Between the perception of an injustice, and the ability to remove it there is a world of difference, and although we may be unable to remedy the defect the defect remains.

But, indeed, human nature does try to produce a world in which such happenings as those depicted shall either not occur or their consequences shall be reduced to a minimum. We do not hang a son for his parents' crime, nor do humane people blame children for the shortcomings of their parents. To some extent we try to correct the consequences that follow, and even though the endeavor be futile, that is in itself an indictment of the existing order. Man does at least try to correct the injustices his God is said to have created.

It is overlooked also that the evils which follow from wrong actions are not confined to those immediately connected, and who may conceivably have their resentment to some extent dulled, if not lessened, by that fact. People in no way connected, and who can have no perception of the cause of their suffering, who are unconscious of everything, save the one fact that they are suffering, feel its consequences. When a great war spreads devastation all over the world, can it be said that any useful purpose is served by the sufferings of millions who are not in the slightest degree aware of the cause of their agony? When a shady financial operation brings an innocent man to ruin, and effects all the consequences which Canon Green imagines resulting from the defaulting parent, how can it be said that the catastrophe admits of ethical justification? In many cases the thought of the injury experienced acts itself as a fresh cause of degradation. It creates a rankling and a bitterness which depresses and inhibits the power to struggle, unless it be the desire to struggle for revenge against a condition of things of which the evil results are only too apparent. People are not merely punished for the evil they do; they are punished for the evil that others do, and the punishment, so far as we can see, bears no observable relation to the wrong done. There is no *ethical* relation between actions and consequences. Not alone is the incidence of an action dependent upon personal qualities— some will suffer more from having accidentally told an untruth than others will suffer from having committed gross and deliberate fraud—but nature is absolutely careless of whether what I do is motivated by good or bad intentions. If I get a wetting through going out to help some one in distress, the consequences will be exactly the same as though I had got wet going out to commit a burglary or a murder. And when Dr. Martineau talks of the "natural penalties for guilt," and adds that "sin being there, it would be simply monstrous that there should be no suffering and would fully justify the despair which now raises its sickly cry of complaint against the retributory wretchedness of human transgression" (*Study* II., p. 106), the reply is that there are no such things as "*natural* penalties for guilt." There are only consequences of actions, and they are the same whatever be the moral quality of the actions performed. In the same way that nature may in the course of an earthquake destroy the homes of a dozen worthy families and leave a gambling hell untouched, so it will in other directions punish where a man, from good intentions, places himself in the path of punishment, and refrain from afflicting one whose selfishness or greed has guarded him against attack. There are natural consequences of actions, there are no natural penalties for guilt, and there are no natural rewards for innocence. Rewards and penalties are the creation of man, and it is only in the form of a figure of speech that we can apply them to nature.

It is equally idle to speak of pain as a form of discipline. Professor Sorley says that if the pain in the world can be turned to the increase of goodness, then its existence offers no insuperable objection to "the ethical view of reality." So Dr. Martineau says that suffering is "the moral discipline" through which our nature arrives at its "true elevation." It is needless to multiply quotations; such statements are the commonplaces of theistic controversy, and almost any book that one cares to pick up will supply further illustrations, if they be required. None can reject them, because no theist can afford to candidly admit that the world we know offers no justification for his belief. The belief in the goodness of God, as Canon Green says, is a belief that is "absolutely fundamental to all religion," and if the facts as we see them do not support the belief, some apology must be found that will marry the theory to the fact.

Nevertheless, the belief in the disciplinary power of pain or suffering is, if not quite illusory, so nearly so that it is useless for the purpose for which it is brought forward. In the first place, it does not require very profound study to see that

102

whatever are the lessons taught by suffering they are seldom proportionate to the conduct which cause them, nor do those who suffer reap the alleged disciplinary benefit of their suffering. Let us take a common case. A mother goes out and leaves a child near an unguarded fire. The mother returns to find the child burned to death. Where is the discipline here? Certainly the child cannot have gained any. But there is, of course, the mother. The mother has learned such a lesson that she will never forget it, and will never again commit the same blunder. There we have it. A child is allowed to die by a hideously cruel death in order that a mother may learn a lesson in carefulness. It is good to learn from other sources that God's ways are not our ways. A man who tried to imitate them, and who burned one of his children in order to teach its mother how to look after the rest, would soon find himself in the criminal court, or in an asylum. But what would be insanity or criminal cruelty in the case of man, becomes, in the alembic of religious apologetic, goodness and wisdom in God.

The theory that it is the function of pain to elevate and to discipline is simply not true. One has only to look to see that in countless cases the effect of pain is disaster. The world's best work is not born of pain but of pleasure. There is no pain and no suffering, there is hardly even toil, in the work of a genius. In all the higher walks of music, of art, of literature, the work is perfect in proportion as the worker finds himself in agreeable and pleasant surroundings. And what is true of the higher aspect of art is true also of life in general. Life may be lived in spite of pain, as good work may be done in spite of discouraging circumstances, but one might as well talk of a plant flourishing because of poor soil, or sharp frosts, as to speak of life becoming better because of pain.

The normal function of pain is to depress, that of pleasure is to heighten. As Spencer said, every pain lowers the tide of life;

103

every pleasure raises the tide of life. It is one of the commonest of sights to see those suffering from illness becoming more self-centered, less careful of others, and to see the disintegrating consequences of disease on character. Here and there one may find a character that has had its rough edges smoothed down by suffering, but for every case of that kind one may find a score of an opposite order. It is not the underfed, badly clothed, neglected child that is likely to make the best citizen, but the one that has the best chance of developing itself in healthy surroundings. And it is a curious commentary, if it were true, to argue that a good and wise God so arranged things that pain and suffering, even undeserved suffering, should be the main way for the development of character.

A strange but not uncommon argument is used by Canon Green in dealing with the suffering incidental to the various disasters that overtake mankind from time to time. Suffering, he says, has a certain element of martyrdom about it. Even evils due to human greed and carelessness bring some benefit in their train. Thus, apropos of the *Titanic* disaster:—

Every such disaster tends to produce some improvement for future generations. Ship owners are forced to supply more boats, wireless installment is required on all ships; the idle rich are led to think less of saving useless time and more of saving lives, their own and those of men in the stokeholds. In a sense those who perish may be said to be unwilling martyrs who by their deaths purchase some advantage for others. It will be said that it is a great price to pay for a small advantage, and one which might have been cheaply gained in some other ways. That is so. But so too the ways of nature are cruel. So many seeds must be sown, so many young animals or birds or fishes born, so many must be trampled out of existence, that only the best may survive. (*Problem of Evil*; pp. 163-4).

That certainly puts all the owners of slum property, all the grasping ship-owners, all those who batten and fatten on other people's welfare in a most favorable light. We have been thinking them almost criminals when they were in reality public benefactors. They lead to many improvements, and even though the improvements come too late to benefit those who suffer from the evils, yet they do come—sometimes. Certainly it might give some comfort if the sufferers knew what it was they were being sacrificed for, and that others would be benefited by their death. But they do not, and we are therefore bound to conclude that whatever satisfaction is felt is by those who survive. When a *Titanic* sinks it must be the people on shore who see the element of goodness in it since it makes travelling easier for *them*. And the kindness developed in one who can excuse the brutalities of nature because it brings some benefit to himself is of a rather startling nature.

The fundamental fault in all reasoning of this order lies in the assumption that pain ceases to be pain if it can be shown to bring good to *some* one. But that it not so. Pleasure and pain are not quantitative things, increments of which can be carried on from generation to generation and a balance struck at the end, much as one strikes a balance between the profits and losses of a year's trading. All suffering and all enjoyment are of necessity personal. Suffering is not increased by extending it over a million instances. There was not more pain because a larger number happened to be be killed in the European war than are killed in a borderland skirmish. There were a larger *number* of people involved in the one case than in the other, but that is all. Multiplying the number of cases makes a greater appeal to a sluggish imagination, but it adds nothing substantial to the fact. Feeling, whether it be pleasant or painful, is a matter of individual experience, and that being so it is not the number of people who suffer through no fault of their own, and, so far as one can see, without any benefit proportionate to the suffering experienced, but the fact of there being this suffering at all. That is the point the theist must face; it is the one point he systematically avoids.

Another form of the same argument meets us in the familiar plea that bodily pain "sounds the alarm bell of disease in time for its removal." In some sense it may be admitted that a painful feeling, in certain circumstances, does act as a warning that persistence will lead to disaster. But it is not universally true in the sense and in the degree that is needed to justify the argument, and it is a "warning" out of all proportion to the danger faced. In the first place, pain cannot be a warning against disease, it can only be an indication of its presence. It does not warn us against the dangers of a contemplated course of conduct, nor can it tell us what conduct has led to the pain experienced. And in the case of contagious diseases, what amount of warning is there given? In some case the victim is stricken and is dead in so short a time as not to know with what it is he has been afflicted, and certainly without any chance of being warned. What warning is there in the case of a violent poison? Or what relation is there between pains felt and dangers run? The most dangerous diseases may have painless beginnings, and be well rooted in the system before the victim is driven by discomfort to seek medical advice. On the other hand, a corn or a toothache, neither of them very deadly ailments, create pain out of all proportion to their gravity. And if we take the case of excessive cold we have here an instance where instead of pain acting as a warning, the danger just acts as an anesthetic. The victim is oppressed by drowsiness, sinks into insensibility, finally death. Here it is not the approach of death that is painful, but the return to life, the pain of restoring circulation being very severe indeed.

Fear, which may be classed as a species of pain, appears to act, in the majority of instances, as an enemy, rather than as a friend to the animal experiencing it. Thus Professor Mosso points out that in the animal organism there exists a number of harmful reactions that increase in number the graver the peril becomes. We have all read of the "fascination" of the bird by the serpent, and there are other animals that in the presence of an enemy become so palsied with fear as to become incapable of defense, even that of flight. And with man it is not as the danger becomes most acute that his nerves become steadier and his courage firmer. The opposite is probably more often the case. In all these cases it is as though nature had lured the animal or man into a position of grave danger, and then does its best to divest him of adequate means of defense against it.

Common sense revolts against the doctrine that pain is a good thing, and the fact of this is everywhere seen in the attempt of man to get rid of it. No one trusts it as a sure warning against disease; no one turns to it as a means of purifying character. All these pleas are the mere platitudes of a religious apologetic trying to harmonize a primitive theory of things with a larger knowledge and a more developed moral sense. Pain and suffering in the world remain facts whether we believe in the existence of a God or not, but we are at least freed from the paralyzing horror of the belief that all the suffering and pain in nature is part of a plan. If man realized all that that belief involved it might indeed rob his mind of all strength to struggle against the forces that make for his destruction. Fortunately no race of people could act upon the logical implications of the theistic theory and maintain its existence. In practice, as well as in theory, theism has had to come to terms with facts. And now the series of adjustments have almost reached their end. The belief in God has been traced to its origin, and we know it to have issued in an altogether discredited view of the world and of man. We know that man does not discover God, he invents him, and an invention is properly discarded when a better instrument is forthcoming.

To-day the hypothesis of God stands in just the same relation to the better life of to-day as the fire drill of the savage does to the modern method of obtaining a light. The belief in God may continue awhile in virtue of the lack of intelligence of some, of the carelessness of others, and of the conservative character of the mass. But no amount of apologizing can make up for the absence of genuine knowledge, nor can the flow of the finest eloquence do aught but clothe in regal raiment the body of a corpse.

Part II

SUBSTITUTES FOR ATHEISM

Chapter X

A Question of Prejudice

It affords some ground for surprise that there should be so great a resentment shown against religious disbelief in general and against Atheism in particular. We have here more than the mere rejection of a theory or view of life. There is a certain emotional resentment, a shrinking from the one who is guilty of disbelief, such as is not explainable on ordinary grounds. The attitude is ridiculous, so ridiculous that many who adopt it are ashamed to openly acknowledge it, but it is there, and its existence calls for explanation.

We believe this is to be found in the peculiar history of the god-idea combined with primitive theories of social life. Like many frames of mind that persist in civilized society, this attitude towards disbelief has its roots in a conception of the world that has been generally discarded and in social conditions that have ceased to exist among civilized people. To begin with, we have the fact that religion dominates the life of primitive man to a degree that is almost inconceivable to the modern mind. The anger of the tribal gods has to be always reckoned with. What they desire must be done, what they do not desire must be avoided. In the next place there exists a very strong sense of collective responsibility. What one member of a tribe does the whole of the tribe is responsible for, both to the members of other tribes and to the gods. We see a survival of this in the reversion to a more primitive state of things that takes place during a war. In some circumstances hatred of the whole of a people with whom a nation is at war becomes a duty, and all are responsible for the offences of each. So in primitive times an offence against the gods became an act of treason against the tribe. It might expose the whole of the tribe to disaster.

It is not, it must be noted, that primitive man is fond of the gods, or jealous of their honor; he is not any more fond of them than is the modern citizen of the tax-collector. And no one will ever really understand the question of religion until he rids himself of the notion that primitive man spends his time *looking* for gods or that he is happy in their company. He is simply afraid that a single unruly member may get the whole tribe into a serious difficulty. The savage is severely practical; his conduct rests upon grounds of, to him, the most obvious utility, and his treatment of the heretic leaves little to be desired on the score of effectiveness. The unbeliever is a dangerous person, and he is promptly suppressed. The first heretic died a martyr to the tribe; the last heretic will die a martyr to the race.

Primitive conditions die out, but primitive feelings linger, and although in theory we have reached the stage of believing that each person must bear the consequences of his own religious opinions, the deeply rooted dislike to the man who rejects the rule of the gods remains.

Historically we have also to reckon with the operations of an interested priesthood, but leaving that on one side as a secondary development it would seem that one must trace to some such cause as the one above indicated the deep and widespread dislike to such a term as atheism, even by many who to all intents and purposes are atheist in their opinion. Certainly in this country, where compromise is more fashionable than in many other places, the dislike to the word is partly due to its uncompromising character. It is clear cut and definite. Its connotations cannot be misunderstood by any one who takes the word in its literal meaning. The Theist is one who believes in a personal God. The Atheist is one who is without belief in a personal God. The meaning is clear, and the implied mental attitude is plain. It is opposed to theism, and has no significance apart from Theism. And, as will be seen, when non-theists quarrel with it, it is only because it is miss-stated or misunderstood.

But most people dislike clear cut terms. They prefer to exist in an atmosphere of mental ambiguity and intellectual fog which blurs outlines and obscures differences. Unbeliever is preferable to some, skeptic—presumably because of its age and philosophical associations, is a greater favorite, and Agnostic is more beloved than either—the latter has indeed been pressed into the service of a more or less nebulous "religion." As it is said, "We are all Socialists nowadays," so it is said that we are unbelievers or Agnostics nowadays. But no one says we are all Atheists nowadays. Timidity can find no use for a word of that character. Of course, if a man believes that some word other than Atheism best describes his state of mind, he has a perfect right to select the one that seems fittest. But when one finds non-theists repudiating the name of Atheist with as much moral indignation as though they had been accused of shoplifting, one cannot help the suspicion that the heat displayed is not unconnected with some lurking fear of the "respectabilities." It does seem that while many may have outgrown all fear of the God of orthodoxy, the fear of the god of social pressure remains.

So far as the Theist is concerned it is quite understandable that his objection to Atheism should involve a certain moral element. That would result from what has already been said concerning the cause of the fear of heresy. Still one would have thought that in these days it would require a person of almost abnormal stupidity to assume that disbelief in God has its roots in a defective moral character. The facts would warrant a quite opposite conclusion. In the first place, the rejection of any well-established belief argues a degree of independence of mind that is, unfortunately, not common. The ordinary mind follows the common route. It is the extraordinary mind that strikes out from the beaten path. The heretic, whether in politics or in religion, may be wrong, but there is always with him the guarantee of a certain measure of mental strength that is not, on the face of the matter, present with one who follows the orthodox path. And that in itself represents a type of mind of no little social value. Moreover, I for one, am quite ready to assert that, class for class, the Freethinker does represent a type of mind considerably above the average. That this is not more generally recognized is due to the policy of the religious advocate in contrasting the uneducated Freethinker with the educated believer.

Secondly, it strikes one as almost insane to assume that in a Christian country Atheism should be professed as a cloak or as an excuse for misconduct. They who talk in this strain greatly undervalue the accommodating power of religion. Is there a single form of rascality known to man for which religion has not been able to provide a sanction? If there is I have failed to come across it. The use of religion made by tyranny in all ages and in all countries is proof of how accommodating it is to man's passions and interests. The picture of the dying murderer meeting his end, filled with the consolation of religion, and certain of his speedy salvation, contains a lesson that all may read if they will.

Error there may be in any case where opinion is concerned, but profession of an opinion that paves the way for suspicion and persecution provides a *prima facie* guarantee of honesty that cannot be furnished by the advocacy of one that stands high in the public favor. For aught I know to the contrary, every one of England's Bishops may be quite honest men. But there can be no certainty about it so long as the profession carries with it all it does. The dice are loaded in favor of conviction. But the man who faces social ostracism, and even loss of liberty in defense of an opinion, is giving a hostage to truth such as none other can give.

This association of heresy with a defective moral character is a very old game. It has been played by all religions, and, it must be admitted, with considerable success. Writing in the second century Lucian shows us the same policy at work in his day. In one of his dialogues, when the Atheist has refuted one after another the theistic arguments of his opponent, the defender of the gods turns on his opponent with—

You god robbing, shabby, villainous, infamous, halter-sick vagabond! Does not everybody know that your father was a tatterdemalion, and your mother no better than she should be? that you murdered your brother and are guilty of other execrable crimes? You lewd, lying, rascally, abominable varlet.

That type of disputant is still with us, and is still supporting his beliefs with the same tactics. And it is successful with some. There is a certain snobbishness in human nature that makes it seek the association of well-known names and shun all of those with an unfashionable reputation. To observe the way in which some people will introduce into their conversation, speeches, or writings, the names of well-known men, is a revelation of this mental snobbery. And the moral equivalent of this is the fear of being found in the company of an opinion that has been branded as immoral. Such people have all the fear of an unpopular opinion that a savage has of a tribal taboo—it is, in fact, a survival of the same spirit that gave the tribal taboo its force. It is, thus, not a very difficult matter to warn people off an undesirable opinion. Samuel Taylor Coleridge relates how the clergy raised the cry of Atheism against him, although he had never advanced further than Deism. And it is to his credit that in referring to this charge he said:—

Little do these men know what Atheism is. Not one man in a thousand has either strength of mind or goodness of heart to be an Atheist. I repeat it. Not one man in a thousand has either strength of mind or goodness of heart to be an Atheist.

And we have also the oft-quoted testimony of the late Professor Tyndall:—

It is my comfort to know that there are amongst us many whom the gladiators of pulpit would call Atheists and Materialists, whose lives, nevertheless, as tested by any accessible standard of morality would contrast more than favorably with the lives of those who seek to stamp them with this offensive brand. When I say "offensive," I refer merely to the intention of those who use such terms, and not because Atheism or Materialism, when compared with many of the notions ventilated in the columns of religious newspapers has any particular offensiveness to me. If I wish to find men who are scrupulous in their adherence to engagements, whose words are their bond, and to whom moral shiftiness of any kind is subjectively unknown, if I wanted a loving father, a faithful husband, an honorable neighbor, and a just citizen, I would seek him among the band of Atheists to which I refer. I have known some of the most pronounced amongst them, not only in life, but in death—seeing them approaching with open eyes the inexorable goal, with no dread of a "hangman's whip," with no hope of a heavenly crown, and still as mindful of their duties, as if their eternal future depended upon their latest deeds.

Still the moral cry is too useful with the crowd to lead to the conviction that anything one could say would lead to its disuse. In the dialogue of Lucian's to which we have referred, and after the theist has been refuted by the Atheist, Hermes consoles the chief deity, Zeus, by telling him that even though a few may have been won over by the arguments of the Atheist, the vast majority, "the whole mass of uneducated Greeks and the Barbarians everywhere," still remain firm in their faith. And although Zeus replies that he would prefer one sensible man to a thousand fools, when a case depends upon the adherence of the relatively foolish, numbers will always bring some consolation to the champions of an intellectually distressed creed.

Chapter XI

What is Atheism?

Between Atheism and Theism there is no logical halting place. But there are, unfortunately, many illogical ones. Few possess the capacity for pushing their ideas to a logical conclusion, and some position is finally discovered which has the weakness of both extremes with the strength of neither. With many there is vague talk of a "Power" manifested in the universe, and by giving this the dignity of capital letters it is evidently hoped that ether people will recognize it as an equivalent for God. But power, with or without capitals, is not God. It is not the existence of a "Power" that forms the kernel of the dispute between the Theist and the Atheist, but what that power is like. The issue arises on the point of whether it is personal or not. That it is, is what the religious man believes. As Mr. Balfour says, when the plain man speaks of God he means "a God whom men can love, to whom men can pray, who takes sides, who has purposes and preferences, whose attributes, however conceived, leaves the possibility of a personal relation between Himself and those whom he has created." ("Theism and Humanism," p. 21.) What the genuine believer has in view is not the worthless abstraction of a rationalized metaphysic, but the personal being of historic theology.

117

It is now my purpose to take a few of these substitutes for Atheism by the aid of which some persons seek to mark themselves off from a declared and reasoned unbelief. As outstanding examples of this one may take two men of no less eminence than Herbert Spencer and Professor Huxley. Both of these men have rendered great service to advanced thought, but both have only succeeded in repudiating Atheism by misstating and misrepresenting it. In addition to the service that Spencer unwittingly rendered the current religion by his use of the "Unknowable" (with which we deal fully later), a further help was given by his destruction of an Atheism that had no existence. This remarkable performance will be found in the first part of his "First Principles." Respecting the origin of the universe, he tells us, there are three intelligible propositions—although neither of these, on his own showing, is intelligible. We may assert that it is self-existent, that it is self-created, or that it is created by an external agency. All three propositions, he proceeds to show, are equally inconceivable. The noticeable thing about the performance is that Atheism is identified with the proposition that the universe is self-existent. A very slight acquaintance with the writings of representative Atheists would have shown Mr. Spencer that "the origin of the universe" is one of those questions on which Atheism has wisely been silent, and it has also insisted that all attempts to deal with such a question can only result in a meaningless string of words. To the Atheist, "the universe"—the sum of existence—is a fact that no amount of reasoning can get behind or beyond. To think of the universe as a whole is an impossibility; while to talk of its origin is to assume, first, that it did originate, and, second, that we have some means by which we can transcend all the known limits of the human mind. The Atheist can say, and has said, with Mr. Spencer himself— whose final statement of Agnosticism differs in no material respect from Atheism, that in discussing the "origin of the

118

universe," we can only succeed in multiplying impossibilities of thought "by every attempt we make to explain its existence." No one has pointed out more clearly than Mr. Spencer that "infinity" is not a conception, but the negation of one. The pity is that he did not realize that in taking up this position he was on exactly the same level of criticism that Atheists have pursued. For them the universe is an ultimate fact; all that we can do is to mark the ceaseless changes always going on around us, and to develop our capacity for modifying their action in the interests of human welfare. Farther than this our knowledge does not and cannot go; and it may be added that even though our knowledge could go beyond the world of phenomena, such knowledge would not be of the slightest possible value.

It may also be pointed out that, just as it is not true that Atheism attempts to explain the origin of the universe, so it is unfair to tie the Atheist down to any particular theory of cosmic evolution. As a mental attitude Atheism is quite independent of any theory of cosmic working, so long as that theory does not involve an appeal to deity. As we shall see, Atheism, from the point of view both of history and etymology, stands for the negation of theism, and its final justification must be found in the un-tenability of the theistic position.

Rightly enough it may be argued that the acceptance of Atheism implies a certain general mental attitude towards both cosmic and social questions, but the Atheist, as such, is no more committed to a special scientific theory than he is committed to a special theory of government. Of course, it is convenient for the Theist to first of all saddle his opponent with a set of social or scientific beliefs, and then to assume that in attacking those beliefs he is demolishing Atheism, but it is none the less fighting on a false issue. All that Atheism necessarily involves is that all forms of Theism are logically untenable, and consequently the only effective method of destroying Atheism is to establish its opposite.

Professor Huxley's treatment of Atheism proceeds on similar lines to that already dealt with, but is more elaborate in character. Discussing the nature of his own opinions he repudiates all sympathy with Atheism, because:

"the problem of the ultimate cause of existence is one which seems to me to be hopelessly out of reach of my poor powers. Of all the senseless babble I have ever had occasion to read, the demonstrations of those philosophers who undertake to tell us about the nature of God would be the worst, if they were not surpassed by the still greater absurdities of the philosophers who try to prove there is no God." (*On the Hypothesis the Animals are Automata.*)

And on another occasion, replying to a correspondent, he expresses the opinion that "Atheism is, on philosophical grounds, untenable, that there is no evidence of the god of the theologians is true enough, but strictly scientific reasoning can take us no further. When we know nothing we can neither affirm nor deny with propriety." (*Life and Letters*, p. 162.)

Here, again, we have the common error that Atheism seeks in some way to explain the ultimate cause of existence. And this in spite of continuous disclaimers that all search for a "first cause," or for a "cause of existence" is midsummer madness. The fault here, we suspect, is that both writers took their statement of Atheism, not from Atheistic writers but from their opponents. But it is none the less surprising that it was not recognized that both "a first cause" and an "ultimate cause of existence," are, strictly speaking, theistic questions. I do not mean that these questions may not suggest themselves to non-theists, but that when they are raised clearly and definitely they are seen to belong to a class of questions to which no rational answer is possible. To the Theist, however, the questions arise from his primary assumptions. His theory is one of final causes; his deity is postulated as the cause of existence, and he cannot give up the questions as hopeless without admitting his position to be indefensible. It is quite usual for the theist to propound problems which only arise on his own assumptions, and then call upon his opponents for answers to them, but there is no justification whatever for non-theists playing the same game. Atheism has nothing to do with final causes, and therefore is not concerned with defending its illogicalities. Theism is a doctrine of final causes, and in arguing that it is absurd to express an opinion upon the subject Professor Huxley was adding a good reason in support of the position he believed himself to be destroying.

Huxley's other objection to Atheism is that it perpetuates the absurdity of trying to prove there is no God. How far is that true? Or in what sense is it true? The danger in all discussion on this point lies in our taking it for granted that "God" conveys a definite and identical meaning to all people. But this is very far from being the case. What anyone means by "God" it is impossible to say until some further description has been given. When this has been done, and not until then, "God" may become the subject of affirmation or denial. Until then we are playing with empty words. By itself "God" means nothing. It offers the possibility of neither negation nor affirmation.

Now Professor Huxley would have readily admitted that the truth of a proposition may be denied whenever its terms involve a contradiction. And the ground of this is the sheer impossibility of bringing the terms together in thought. That a circle may be square, or that parallel lines may enclose a space, are propositions the truth of which may be denied offhand. The ground of this is that the conception of squareness and circularity, of straight lines and an enclosed space are mutually destructive, they cancel each other. And so far as Atheism may be said to involve the denial of particular gods that denial is based upon precisely similar grounds. When defined it is seen that the attributes of this defined god cancel each other as effectually as squareness rules out the idea of a circle; either this or they are simply unthinkable. You cannot have an infinite personality any more than you can have a six-sided octagon, nor can you posit an infinite personality without divesting the terms of all meaning.

It may also be noted in passing that both the theist and the Agnostic actually do deny the existence of particular gods without the least hesitation. No rational Agnostic would hesitate to deny the existence of Jupiter, Javeh, Allah, or Brahma. No Christian would hesitate to deny the existence of the gods of a tribe of savages. Even believers in the current theology have evolved beyond the stage of the primitive Christians, who accepted the existence of the Pagan deities with the proviso that they were demons. And it is a mere verbal quibble to say that these people merely deny each other's conception of deity. Each man's conception of god *is* his god, and to say that no being answering to that conception exists is to say that his god does not exist, and in relation to the god denied the denier is in exactly the position in which he places the Atheist.

So far then the Atheism of each is just a question of degree or of relation. So far as Atheism involves the denial of deity the follower of one religion is an Atheist in relation to the followers of every other religion. Each religion—among civilized people—is atheistic from the standpoint of the followers of other gods. The affirmation of one god involves the denial of other gods. This would really seem to be the historical significance of the term. The early Christians were called atheists by the Pagans, and some of them accepted it without demur. At a later date Spinoza, Voltaire, Paine, and others were called atheists, and the epithet has lost its force to-day only because the evolution of thought has broken down many religious barriers, and is rapidly dividing people into two groups—those who believe in some god and who believe in none at all. Now all that Atheism—conscious and reflective Atheism—does is to carry a step further the restricted denial of the ordinary religionist. The Christian theist denies every god but his own. The Atheist, seeing no more evidence for the existence of the Christian deity than for the existence of any of the deities discarded by the Christian, seeing, further, that there are exactly the same contradictions involved in assuming the existence of any one of the world's deities, places the Christian deity on the list as among those gods in whose existence he does not believe, and whose existence, so far as it is defined, may be logically denied.

The really distinguishing feature of philosophic Atheism is its comprehensiveness, the ranking of all known deities, big and little, ancient and modern, savage and civilized, gross and subtle, upon the same level. Historically, we see them all originating in the same conditions, passing through substantially the same phases of development, finally to meet with the same fate as civilization develops. In this respect Atheism has to be considered in its historic developments. It begins, as we have seen in the rejection of a particular god, in favor of some other deity. It is only at a very much later stage that the whole idea of god is subjected to examination and analysis in such a way as to lead to the rejection of the conception of god as a whole. But with that aspect of the subject we shall be concerned later.

But does Atheism deny the existence of any possible god? This question might admit of a simple answer if one only knew

123

precisely what it meant. It is easy enough to understand what is meant by God so long as we keep to any or all of the gods of the world's religions. But what is meant by god standing alone and undefined? Historically "God" means a deity believed in by some people, some where, at some time. And if we put on one side these particular gods we have nothing left that can be either affirmed or denied. God in the abstract is not a real existence any more than tree in the abstract is a real existence. There is a pine tree, a pear tree, an apple tree, etc., but there is and can be no "tree" apart from some particular tree. So with "god." There are particular gods, but if we do away with these, we have no god left as a separate existence. "God" then becomes a mere word conveying no meaning whatever. Atheism does not deny the existence of *a* god for the same reason that it does not deny the existence of Abracadabra—both terms mean as much, or as little. And it is more than absurd for people who have rejected theism to continue using the word "god" as though it had a quite definite meaning apart from the gods of the various theologies. We have Professor Huxley admitting that "there is no evidence of the existence of the god of the theologians," and we imagine that he would have met the affirmation of their existence with a flat contradiction. At any rate he would have been quite justified in doing so. But when he asserts, with a show of logical precision, but in reality with great looseness, that "it is preposterous to assert that there is no god because he cannot be such as we think him to be," he is using language for which no precise meaning can be found. To be intelligible, the sentence implies that we have some conception answering to the terms used, and this, as we have pointed out with almost wearisome insistence, is not the case. It is not a case of saying to the theist, "I fully understand your hypothesis, but as at present I do not see enough evidence to convince me of its truth or to demonstrate its error I must suspend judgment." We do *not*

124

understand it. And when we seek to we discover that the terms of the proposition we are asked to accept refuse to be brought together within the compass of a single conception. Suspended judgment where the subject under discussion is understandable is right and proper, but it is quite out of place, and indeed cannot exist, where the proposition before us is void of meaning. In such circumstances suspended judgment is absurd, and it may be added that the affirmation or negation of such a proposition is absurd likewise.

Only one other word need be said on this point. It may be urged that educated believers mean by "God" not the anthropomorphic deity of the theologies, but a personal intelligence controlling things. But this is really not less anthropomorphic than the form in which the god idea meets us in the popular theologies. Its anthropomorphism is only, to unobservant minds, less apparent. The conception of an intelligent, personal being controlling nature is not fundamentally less objectionable than the frankly man-like being of the early theologies. Intelligence, as we know it (and to talk of an intelligence that is unlike the intelligence we know is absurd) is as much a characteristic of human, or animal, organization, as arms and legs are. Mind, after all, is only known to us as a function of an organism. That it is more than this, or other than this, is a pure assumption. And to divest "God" of all physical parts, while retaining his functions, is sheer nonsense. There is the personal intelligence of Smith, or Brown, or Robinson, but it is absurd to wipe out all the particular Smiths, and Browns, and Robinsons, and then talk as though their qualities continue in existence. So with God. If we reject all the gods of the theologies one after another, what god have we left to talk about? All we have left is the memory of a delusion.

It is equally fallacious to talk of "God" as an equivalent of force

125

in the abstract, or as the equivalent of some non-intelligent force. This is not what people ever meant, or mean, by god. What religious folk believe in, what they pray to, is a person who can hear them, and who can do things. A god only dimly apprehended may be tolerated, but for how long will faith continue to worship an existence that can neither do nor hear nor sympathize? There is a limit to even religious folly. And even a savage only worships "sticks and stones" *after* he endows them with life and intelligence.

Finally, if there is one thing clear to the modern mind it is that science has no room in its theory of things for an over-ruling intelligence. Sir Oliver Lodge well sums up the attitude of science in the following sentences:—"Orthodox science shows us a self-contained and self-sufficient universe, not in touch with anything above or beyond itself—the general trend and outline of it known—nothing supernatural or miraculous, no intervention of beings other than ourselves, being conceived possible." (*Man and the Universe*, p. 14, Popular ed.) Personally, we question whether there are any scientists of repute who really believe in the existence of a personal intelligence above or beyond nature. Some may make professions to the contrary, but it will usually be found that the qualifications introduced rob their professions of all value. Certainly their teaching is destitute of any such conception. Modern scientific thought leaves no room for the operations of deity. The miraculous is generally discarded. Response to prayer is whittled down to a species of self-delusion, to be valued on account of its subjective influence only. The scientific theory of things, incomplete as it may be in many of its details, leaves no room for the operations of a god. Not alone does it leave no room for a god, but if the scientific conception of the world is to stand, then it would be necessary to repeat Bakunine's *mot*, and to say, "If there were a god it would be necessary to destroy him." You simply cannot have at one and the same time a universe in which all that occurs is the consequence of calculable and indestructible forces, the operations of which can be foreseen and relied upon, and a universe controlled by a self-determining deity, capable of modifying the action of these same forces. You may have one or the other, but it is sheer lunacy to imagine that you can have both. Either uniformity with invariable causation, or a world in which every scientific calculation must be prefaced with the "D.V." of a prayer meeting. And the Atheist, who accepts the principles of modern science, says, not merely that he is without a belief in god, but that he fails to see any necessity for his existence, or anything for him to do if he did exist. He passes the gods of the world in review and categorically dismisses each one as a myth. In doing this he has the concurrence of all theists in discarding every god save one—his own. The Atheist simply applies the same rule to each, and metes out the same judgment to all.

Chapter XII

Spencer and the Unknowable

We have already referred to the use made by religionists of Spencer's "Unknowable." This theory was not without its forerunners, and in England was already in the field in the teachings of Hamilton and Mansel. Spencer gave it a still greater vogue. As he presented it, it came before the world with all the prestige attaching to its association with one of the most comprehensive of modern thinkers, and one of the most influential in the schools of evolutionary philosophy. It was also connected with a world theory that claimed to be strictly scientific in its character. It became not only a fashion in certain circles, it founded a school, and gained numerous followers in the religious world. Its author propounded it as a basis on which to reconcile religion and science, and many were ready to accept it as such. Printed in all the glory of capital letters, appearing sometimes as "The Ultimate Reality," sometimes as the "Unconditioned," sometimes as an "Infinite and Eternal Energy," it was equally impressive under all its forms. It provided just that solemn kind of formula that the religious mind is accustomed to hear, and if it was as meaningless as the Athanasian Creed, is was, for that reason, quite as satisfying. It gave all the comfort of a religious confession of faith, and it has been the parent of a whole host of more recent apologies for

God.

In itself the "Unknowable" was harmless enough. Its philosophic value is not great, its scientific utility is nil. To say that everything proceeds from an "Ultimate Reality" is not very helpful, and to follow on with the declaration that we know nothing about it, and that it would be of no use to us if we did, does not sound very encouraging. It reminds one of the description of the horse that had only two faults—one that it was hard to catch, and the other that it was no good when it was caught. We repeat with all solemnity the formula that all things proceed from an infinite and eternal energy, and that this is the Ultimate Reality, and then find that in relation to any and every question we are precisely where we were. Its acceptance in certain religious circles, and its use later, may be taken as evidence of the fact that what the pious mind longs for is not sense but satisfaction.

Still there remains cause for wonder that this "Unknowable" should ever have been taken as affording foundation for the belief in deity. The most extreme materialist or Atheist need not be in the slightest degree disconcerted on being told things proceed from an "Infinite and Eternal Energy." It is only what the Atheist has said, minus the capital letters. He has affirmed his conviction, that all phenomena result from the permutations of matter and force, which are eternal because no time limit can be placed to their operations. And you do not add anything material to the statement by printing it in capital letters. That the Spencerian abstraction should have been taken as a substitute for deity proves how desperate the situation is. Drowning men clutch at straws, and a disintegrating deity hopes to renew his strength by the lavish use of capital letters.

For, after all, what the theist needs is, not an eternal energy, but a personality. An inscrutable existence will not do. There is no dispute that something exists. There is no quarrel over mere existence. It is with the nature of what exists and the mode of its operation that the issue arises. The theist needs a special kind of energy, a special form of existence, a special kind of "reality" if his case is to be established. It will not do for Mr. Spencer to assure him that this "Ultimate Reality" is higher than personal. How Mr. Spencer knows that something, the nature of which is unknown, is higher than something else, is more than one can tell. But that does not matter. Higher or lower, it is all the same. Either way it is different from personal, and if it is different it is not the same, it is not personal. Whatever other qualities this "Ultimate Reality" has or lacks, it must have that one if it is to be of use to the theist. And to say that it is higher than personal is to say that it is not personal at all, and to repeat in a roundabout manner what the Atheist has been saying all the time.

What now is Spencer's theory of an ultimate reality that must for ever remain unknowable? Following a line of thought that had been steadily gaining ground since Hume—although much older than Hume—Spencer holds that in final analysis all our knowledge is a knowledge of mental states and their relations. Beyond this we *know* nothing, and can never know anything. Nevertheless, while we cannot know anything beyond consciousness, the conditions of thinking oblige us to assume that something exists as the cause of our states of mind. Just as black implies something that is not black, hard something that is not hard, so we must conceive, as against the conditioned, relative existence of our conscious states, an unconditioned, absolute existence as their cause. It is this assumed, but completely unknown cause of our conscious states, and of all else, that Spencer distinguishes as the Unknowable, the Unconditioned, the Absolute, etc., and which appears to have brought so much consolation to hard-pressed theists.

I have no intention of discussing here the philosophic value of the "Unknowable." But one may say, in passing, that even from that point of view Spencer is untrue to his own Agnosticism in speaking of the Unconditioned as the *cause* of phenomena. For causation is a category of the conditioned, it belongs to the world we know. It is not something that exists beyond consciousness, it is something that is supplied by consciousness and which possesses validity only within the world of phenomena. On Spencer's own theory of relativity a cause only exists in relation to an effect. Destroy the one and you destroy the other. Thus, if the Unknowable is a cause of phenomena it ceases to be the unconditioned and becomes part of the phenomenal order. If, on the other hand, it is not part of the phenomenal sequence, it cannot stand to phenomena in a genuine casual relation. It is, however, only fair to point out that between the Unknowable and the evolutionary philosophy of Spencer the only connection between them is that they are both in the same work. In all probability it is an unconscious survival of Spencer's earlier theism, which was active at the time the Synthetic Philosophy was originally planned, but which became more and more attenuated as Spencer grew older, and disappears entirely from the more important volumes of the series. And but for the help it has been supposed to give the belief in god, the "Unknowable" would only have ranked as a harmless speculation of no value to anyone or to anything. This is substantially admitted in a postscript to the 1899 edition of "First Principles." At the conclusion of the section entitled "The Unknowable," he says:—

The reader is not called on to judge respecting any of the arguments or conclusions contained in the foregoing five chapters and in the above paragraphs. The subjects on which we are about to enter are independent of the subjects thus far discussed; and he may reject any or all of that which has gone before while leaving himself free to accept any or all of that

131

which is now to come.

In other words, the "Unknowable" is a pure abstraction, having no organic connection with the Synthetic Philosophy, or indeed with any philosophy of value. Mr. Spencer's warning to his readers seems to quite justify Mr. Bradley's rather caustic comment, "I do not wish to be irreverent, but Mr. Spencer's attitude towards his Unknowable strikes me as a pleasantry, the point of which lies in its unconsciousness. It seems a proposal to take something for God simply and solely because we do not know what the devil it can be." (Note to p. 128 of *Appearance and Reality*.)

The curious thing is that Mr. Spencer really offers his readers two theories of the nature of religion. One is contained in his "Principles of Sociology," and so far as it traces all religious ideas to the delusions and illusions of the primitive savage is substantially that held by all modern anthropologists. The other is contained in his "First Principles," and the two theories, like parallel lines, never meet. Though born in the same brain they are quite distinct, and even contradictory.

The substance of this second theory may be summarized as follows:—

1. The conditions of human thought compel the recognition of an unknowable reality of which all phenomena are the expression.

2. The function of religion, from the earliest time, has been the assertion of the existence of an unknowable reality, and to keep alive a consciousness of the insoluble mystery surrounding it.

3. The function of science is to deal with the known and the knowable, with all that is presented in experience, with the

world of phenomena exclusively.

4. Religion having for its subject matter the unknown and unknowable, while science has for its subject matter the known and the knowable, religion and science are not antagonistic, but complementary. Conflicts only arise when one trespasses on the other's department, and a recognition of the true line of demarcation effectually reconciles these hitherto hostile forces.

A very obvious criticism of number one is in affirming a consciousness of an "Unknowable," its quality of unknowableness is annihilated. Existence can only be predicated of that which affects consciousness in some manner; and so far as I have the slightest apprehension or consciousness of anything existing, to that extent it ceases to be the unknowable. Our knowledge of it may be imperfect or altogether erroneous; we may feel it impossible that we should ever rightly understand it; but so far as we think about it we are bound to assimilate it to the best of our knowledge, even though it be only under the category of force. In brief, "unknowableness" is not a property or quality by which a thing may be apprehended; it is a name for complete mental vacuity. It does not refer to the thing itself, it refers only to us. It is a pure negation which Spencer, by sheer verbal play converts into a quasi-positive conception. A consciousness of things unknown can never be more than a consciousness of ignorance. There is only one way to prove the existence of an unknowable, and that is to know nothing about it—not even to know that there is something about which we know nothing.

But, says Spencer, "to say that we cannot know the absolute is, by implication, to affirm that there is an absolute." Certainly, if we take an infirmity of language to be the equivalent of a necessity of existence, not otherwise. When I say that we cannot know a four-sided triangle I do not affirm by implication that a four-sided triangle exists. I am asserting that the phrase, a four-sided triangle, involves conceptions that cannot be brought together in consciousness, and so dismiss it as being without meaning.

The truth is that every one of Spencer's attempts to prove the existence of an unknowable turns out on examination to be no more than a proof of the existence of an unknown, and this is not disputed at any time or by anyone. Thus, after being told that a known cannot be thought of apart from an unknown, we are informed:—

Positive knowledge does not, and never can, fill the whole region of possible thought. At the utmost reach of discovery there arises, and must ever arise, the question, What lies beyond? As it is impossible to think of a limit to space so as to exclude the idea of space lying outside that limit, so we cannot conceive of any explanation profound enough to exclude the question, What is the explanation of the explanation?

With this we can all agree, but it does not bring us any nearer an "unknowable." It is perfectly true that thought can never be comprehensive enough to exhaust the possibilities of existence, since it is of the essence of thinking to limit and define. But it is a sheer impossibility to think of what lies beyond the boundary of our knowledge as unknowable, so far as we think of it at all, we must conceive it as the unknown but possibly knowable. The unknown can only be thought of thus because it is only as it is, by assumption, brought into line with what is already known that it can be thought about at all. We are compelled to think of what lies beyond the limits of our actual knowledge in the same way as a traveler thinks of the fauna and flora of an untraveled country. The new region may present many new features, but until actual observation has taken place, these new features will only be thought of as more or less unusual combinations of known animal and vegetable life. They are substantially identical with what is already known.

No stranger notion ever occurred to a great thinker than that religion and science represent parallel and distinct lines of development, each having its own sphere of operation. It is all the more remarkable when we remember that with Spencer "religion" means all religion, past and present, civilized and savage. And no one is more precise in pointing out how all religious ideas find their beginnings in the conditions of primitive life. And that being the case, one wonders whether we are to picture primitive man as a profound metaphysical philosopher, speculating on that which lies behind phenomena, contemplating an "insoluble Mystery," and paying homage to an "Ultimate Reality"? Nothing could be more absurd. Thinking begins in concrete images, not in abstractions. We have only to note the development of intelligence in children to realize this. And primitive man, not being a mystic nor a metaphysician, bases his religion, not upon a reality that transcends experience, but upon a presumed fact, and what is to him the best known of all facts. And even with modern men it may safely be said that they worship God for what they believe they know about him, not because they believe him to be unknown and unknowable.

Spencer himself may be cited in support of this. In his "Principles of Sociology," where the Unknowable plays no part whatever, he concludes after an elaborate survey of the facts, that the imagination of primitive man is reminiscent, not constructive; his power of thought is feeble, he is without the quick curiosity of civilized man, there is an absence of the conception of causation, he accepts things as they appear, without any vivid desire to inquire into their real nature or their connection with other events, and is without abstract ideas. Clearly, here is not a very promising subject from which

135

to derive even the germ of the idea of a "Reality transcending experience." Spencer also, and quite properly, insists that religious ideas are, under the condition of their origin, national ideas; that we must accept the truth that the laws of thought are everywhere the same, and that, given the data as known to primitive man, the inference drawn by him is a reasonable inference.

With this we agree, but it gives the death blow to the previous statement as to the essential nature of religion, and its essential differentiation from science. For given the constitution of the primitive mind, its ignorance of causation and general lack of knowledge, religion commences not in some search after an eternal reality, but in a natural misunderstanding of observed facts. Primitive religion is just a reasoned misunderstanding of phenomena that in later, and better informed ages, are given an altogether different explanation.

That this is so, Spencer himself makes plain. For he shows, step by step, how the experience of dreams, echoes, shadows, etc., combine to produce the belief in unseen agencies differing in no essential from man save that of possessing greater power and in being invisible. From dreams and other subjective experiences he derives the idea of a double, from death that of a ghost. Hence the ceremonies round the grave, and the attention paid to the double of the dead man, which subsequently develops into ancestor worship. The same train of thought gives a double to objects other than human beings. Hence Animism, Totemism, and their numerous subsidiary developments. Spencer insists, not only that "all religions have a natural genesis," but also that "behind supernatural beings of all orders" there has been in every case a human personality— in other words, every god is developed from a ghost, "ancestor worship is the root of every religion." To this he will admit no exception, and referring to the Jewish religion, he asks contemptuously:—

Must we recognize a single exception to the general truth thus far verified everywhere? While among all races in all regions, from the earliest times down to the present, the conceptions of deities have been naturally evolved in the way shown, must we conclude that a small clan of the Semitic race had given to it supernaturally a conception which, though superficially like the rest, was in substance absolutely unlike them.

And in about half a dozen pages he shows conclusively that the Biblical God had exactly a similar origin to other gods.

Now if this account of religious origins means anything at all (and in spite of differences between anthropologists it is in substance the account of the origin of religion given by all) it means that instead of religion and science moving along parallel lines, religion is simply primitive science. Religion and science, as a very able theistic writer says, "touch and oppose each other as rival methods of explaining, not solely or mainly the life and nature of man, but the universe taken as a whole, man forming a part of it." (W. H. Mallock, *Religion as a Credible Doctrine*, p. ii.) Both are concerned with the same facts, and their respective claims to consideration depend entirely on their ability to explain the facts. For the reasons given by Spencer, man's earliest interpretation of things is inevitably vitalistic. Ghosts—the primitive protoplasm from which the gods are made—are assumed, and once assumed dominate the savage intelligence. Fear combines with ignorance to resist any conception that will wrest power from the hands of these extra-natural agents, "Nature's haughty lords," rule all, and their dynasty is the hardest of all to overthrow.

In spite, however, of all opposition the mechanical theory of things develops, and in developing establishes a clear division between the two conceptions of nature. But the line of demarcation is not that stated by Spencer. Religion no more asserts the existence of an "Unknown Verity," than it asserts a fourth dimension of space. Nor is science concerned with denying the existence of something of which we know nothing, and can never know anything. The essential feature of religion is that it offers a vitalistic explanation of the world as against the mechanical explanation offered by science. And in this religion stands for the earlier as against the later expression of human knowledge. It is the eternal champion of savage thought against civilized intelligence. Its whole significance lies in the persistence of animistic modes of thinking under civilized conditions.

This conclusion, be it observed, is one that is quite borne out by Spencer's own explanation of the nature of religion. Nor do we know of a more remarkable instance of a front rank thinker propounding in one part of his work a theory bearing no relation whatever to the remaining portion, and in addition disproving his own theory at every point.

Spencer's reconciliation of science and religion, which in one form or another is continually in evidence, is only one degree less remarkable than the fact of its being accepted by so many religionists as satisfactory. Following the line of his untenable theory that religion and science pursue parallel lines, he points out that "the agent which has effected the purification (of religion) has been science." That is, the growth of the mechanical theory has driven back the vitalistic one. This is purification only in the sense that a defaulting cashier purifies the firm he robs. "As fact or experience proves that certain familiar changes always happen in the same sequence, there begins to fade from the mind the conception of a special personality to whose variable will they were before ascribed." This process of annexation is, says Spencer, science teaching religion its true function. As a matter of fact, science has given religion no instruction, it has merely issued prohibitions. It has warned religion that there are certain things it must not meddle with, certain departments on which it must not encroach. In this way religion has been forced farther and farther back, until it is left with what? Not with anything that can be known, or is known; it is left supreme in the kingdom of nowhere, ruling over an empire of nothing at all. And so long as religion strives for a more tangible possession so long must there be a conflict between science and religion. But—"as the limits of possible cognition are established, the causes of possible conflict will diminish. And a permanent peace will be reached when science becomes fully convinced that its explanations are proximate and relative; while religion becomes fully convinced that the mystery it contemplates is ultimate and absolute." So, when science has monopolized the entire field of human knowledge, actual and possible, and when religion is satisfied that it knows nothing, and never can know anything of the object of its worship, that it can offer nothing in the shape of counsel or advice, but that its function is to sit in owl-like solemnity, contemplating nothing, meanwhile offering man an eternal conundrum that he must everlastingly give up, then, and not till then, there will be peace between science and religion. And this is called a reconciliation. Mr. Spencer finds two combatants engaged in deadly conflict, he murders one and offers the other the corpse, with the hope that now they will live peacefully together. The scientist is asked to be content with all there is. The religious man is asked to find comfort in the reflection that science must eventually monopolize the entire field of knowledge, but that, in return, religion will be left free to work in an unknowable region, to occupy itself with an unknowable object, and to eternally cry "all is mystery" in an amended philosophic version of the Athanasian Creed.

As a piece of humor this is superb. So also is the following:

"Science has been obliged to abandon the attempt to include within the boundaries of knowledge that which cannot be known, and so has yielded up to religion that which of right belonged to it." Capital! Science gives up to religion that which cannot be known, and as it does not know what it is, that cannot be known, it surrenders to religion absolute vacuity as the proper sphere for its operations. And even this is accompanied with the proviso that if it happens to have made a mistake, the ceded territory will be at once reclaimed. Science would certainly be vindictive if after having murdered religion it declined to live peaceably with its corpse.

The distinction between science and religion is, in truth, neither fundamental nor original. It is one that arises gradually in the history of mental development. And, therefore, when a man such as Professor Arthur Thomson describes religion as being concerned with the recognition of the existence of an independent "spiritual reality," the reply is that religion commences as just an explanation of nature in terms of the then existing knowledge and culture. Religion is just a crude form of science. The separation of the world into a religious and a scientific sphere arises when the religious interpretation of natural happenings gets discredited by advancing knowledge. If one takes such an illustration as that of witchcraft the nature of the process is clear. First we have the interpretation of certain forms of dementia and delusion in terms of religion. Later we have the same facts interpreted in terms of positive knowledge and the religious explanation is rejected. And that, in a sentence is the whole history of religion, once we have cleared away the verbiage with which the subject is surrounded.

The truth of what has just been said is often obscured by unintelligible talk of growth in religion. It is claimed that we acquire truer views of deity, and a process of growth is asserted analogous to that which meets us in knowledge in general. Let us see what truth there is in this.

In ordinary instances when we speak of growth we imply one of three things. Either there is increase in size, or there is an enlargement of function, or there is an increase in knowledge. So long as we keep to these plain meanings of "growth" there can be no confusion. But none of these meanings fit the case of religion. Certainly there has been no increase in the size of religion—it does not, that is, cover a larger area. On the contrary it is continually being warned off more and more territory. It becomes more and more a negligible quantity. One need not go back to primitive times to prove this, any country will supply instances. The displacement of religious by other considerations is observable on all sides.

There has certainly been no growth in the functions exercised by religion. Its function as law-giver in the physical world is now definitely abandoned, and all it asks is that science will let it alone. In ethics and sociology it still maintains a precarious kind of an existence, but it no longer claims supreme power. It is content to urge its utility as a source of inspiration, to rank as one among a number of other forces that are frankly secular in nature. Finally there has been no growth in the shape of an extension of knowledge of the object of religious belief. Of the nature of deity we know no more than did our earliest ancestors. In earlier generations the nature of God, his aims and intentions, were discussed with the same degree of confidence that one now sees displayed in discussing schemes of sanitation. The modern believer is now more anxious to impress upon the world how little he knows about God, or how little it is possible for him to know. This is not surprising except in the fact that it is called religious growth. And if this be a sign of growth one wonders what would be considered indications of decay. Historically religious life presents us, not with a process of growth, but one of shrinkage. To reduce the gods from many to few, and from a few to one is not growth. To limit the functions of deity from those of a direct, particular, and universal character, to an indirect, general form is not growth. To refine the idea of a personal deity until it becomes that of a mere abstract force, is not growth. All these are so many modifications of the religious idea under pressure of advancing knowledge—so many attempts to state religion in such a way that it can conflict with nothing we know to be true because it answers to nothing of which we are certain.

The idea of God, the idea of religion, does not begin in a mystery or in some abstract conception, but in an assumed knowledge of certain concrete facts of experience. Man believes in the gods because of what he thinks he knows about them, not because of what he does not know. The talk of a mystery is the jargon of a priesthood which finds it profitable to keep the lay mind at a distance. Increased emphasis is placed on mystery because religious teachers are alive to the danger of basing their beliefs upon matters that can be brought to the test of experience. Mystery mongering is not the beginning of religion, but a sign of its approaching demise. Mysticism, too, is no more than a cover for a sanctuary that has been emptied of all worthy of respect. But if religion is to really live, it must have some knowledge, no matter how little or how imperfect, of the subject with which it professes to deal. A religion that does not possess this, but is compelled to hand over the whole of life to secular science, signs its own death warrant. It commits suicide to save itself from execution. And as people realize this they turn to clear-eyed science for guidance, leaving religion to such representatives of primitive animism as still survive in a civilized community.

Chapter XIII

Agnosticism

The primary difficulty in dealing with Agnosticism is its elusive character. It is a word of various and vague meanings, and many of those who use it seem to have no great anxiety to fix its meaning with any degree of precision. It is used now in a philosophic and now in a religious sense, and its use in the one connection is justified by its use in another. It has become, in the half century of its existence, as indefinite as "religion," and about as enlightening. On the one side it appears as a counsel of mental integrity with which everyone will agree, and on the other, the religious side, it will vary from a form that is identical, with that much-dreaded "Atheism," to a religious or "reverent" Agnosticism that reminds one—mentally and morally—of Methodism minus its creed. Indeed, to say that a man is an Agnostic nowadays tells one no more than calling a man religious indicates to which one of the world's sects he gives his adherence.

The only aspect of Agnosticism that we are here vitally concerned with is its relation to religion, or specifically with the god-idea. But it will be necessary to say a word, in passing, on at least one other phase.

And first as to the origin of the term. The credit for the first use of the term has always been given to the late Professor Huxley. Mr. R. H. Hutton says that Huxley first suggested the word at a meeting of friends in the house of Mr. James Knowles in 1869. Professor Huxley says that he deliberately adopted it because, "When I reached intellectual maturity and began to ask myself whether I was an atheist, a theist, or a pantheist; a materialist, or an idealist, a Christian, or a freethinker, I found that the more I learned and reflected the less ready was the answer, until at last I came to the conclusion that I had neither art nor part with any of these denominations except the last.... So I took thought and invented what I conceived to be the appropriate title of 'agnostic.'" And he goes on to explain that the term was used as antithetical to the "gnostic" of Church history who knew all about things of which Huxley felt himself in ignorance. To all of which one may say that Huxley appears to have given himself a lot of needless trouble. In philosophy there was the term "Skeptic," and in relation to religion the term "Atheist" was ready to hand. The latter term certainly covered all that Huxley meant by Agnosticism as applied to the god-idea. The plain, and perhaps brutal truth, is that Huxley was just illustrating the fatal tendency of English public men to seek for a label that will mark them off from an unfashionable heresy even more clearly than it separates them from a crumbling orthodoxy. It is certainly suggestive to find, in this connection, a French writer of distinction, M. Emile Boutmy, pointing out that in France, Spencer, Mill, and Huxley would all have been professed atheists. (*The English People*, p. 44.) But Franc is France, and has always possessed the courage to follow ideas to their logical conclusion.

When it comes to a definition of Agnosticism Professor Huxley's position becomes still more difficult of understanding. Agnosticism, he says, is a method the essence of which may be expressed in a single principle. "Positively the

144

principle may be expressed; in matters of the intellect follow your reason so far as it will take you without regard to any other consideration. And negatively; in matters of the intellect, do not pretend that conclusions are certain which are not demonstrated or demonstrable." So far as this goes we have here perfectly sound advice. But why call it Agnosticism? It is no more than the perfectly sound advice that we must be honest in our investigations, and make no claim to certainty where the conditions of certainty do not exist. But we have no more right to call this Agnosticism than we have to give the multiplication table a sectarian or party label.

Nor do we believe for a moment that what Huxley had in view, or what other agnostics have in view, is no more than a counsel of intellectual perfection. What is really at issue here is one's attitude of mind in relation to the belief in God. It is in pretending to know about God that the theist finds himself at issue with the Agnostic, and it is to mark himself off from the theist that the Agnostic gives himself a special label. And the trouble of the Agnostic is that so soon as he begins to justify his position, either he states the atheistic case or he fails altogether to make his case good.

There is, perhaps, one other topic on which agnosticism may be professed, and that is in connection with the question of what is known as the problem of existence. We may profess our belief in the reality of an external world, but deny that any *knowledge* of it is possible. Here we assert that what "substance," or "reality," or "thing in itself," is we do not know and cannot know. But while many attempts are made under the name of "the Absolute," etc., to identify this with "God," it is really nothing of the kind. The belief or disbelief in an external "reality" is a problem in philosophy, it has no genuine connection with theology. To identify the two is a mere dialectical subterfuge. Mere existence is an ultimate fact that must be accepted by all. It is only on the question of its nature that controversy can arise.

Whatever may be claimed on behalf of Agnosticism, it certainly cannot be claimed that it carries a clear and a definite meaning. As we have seen, Professor Huxley used the word to indicate the fact that he was without knowledge of certain things. But what things? To answer that we have to go beyond the word itself—that is, we have to define the definition. As it stands we may profess agnosticism in relation to anything from the prospects of a general election within a given period to the question of whether Mars is inhabited or not. If, then, it is said that what is implied is that the Agnostic is without a knowledge of God, or without a belief in God, the reply is that is exactly the position of the Atheist. And there was no need whatever to coin a new word, if all that was wanted was to express the atheistic position. Still less justifiable was it to proceed to misinterpret Atheism in order to justify a departure that need never have been made.

One cannot at this point forbear a word on Mr.—afterwards Sir—Leslie Stephen's curious justification of his choice of the word Agnosticism. After the enlightening remark that the word "Atheist" carries with it an unpleasant connotation, he says:—

Dogmatic Atheism—the doctrine that there is no God, whatever may be meant by God—is to say the least of it a rare phase of opinion. The word Agnosticism, on the other hand, seems to imply a fairly accurate appreciation of a form of creed already common and daily spreading. The Agnostic is one who asserts—what no one denies—that there are limits to human intelligence. (*An Agnostic's Apology*; p. 1).

And he then goes on to assert that the subject matter of

theology lies beyond these limits.

Now putting on one side this perversion of the meaning of Atheism, was it really worth while to coin a new word to affirm what no one denies? Theists do not deny the limitations of knowledge, on the contrary, they are always affirming it. Neither do all theists deny that "God" is unknowable. That has been affirmed by them over and over again. What they have claimed is that "God" is apprehended rather than known, and they affirm his existence on much the same grounds that others assert the real existence of an external world. Professor Flint's comments on Stephen's performance are quite to the point, and the more noteworthy as coming from a clergyman. He says:

The word Atheist is a thoroughly honest, unambiguous term. It means one who does not believe in God, and it means neither more nor less. It implies neither blame nor approval, neither desert of punishment nor of reward. If a purely dogmatic Atheism be a rare phase of opinion critical Atheism is a very common one, and there is also a form of Atheism which is professedly skeptical or agnostic, but often in reality dogmatic or gnostic. (*Agnosticism*; p. 69).

The more carefully one examines the reasons given for the preference for the word Agnosticism, the clearer it becomes that the real motive is not the wish to obtain mental clarity, but the desire to avoid association with a term that carries, religiously, disagreeable associations. The care taken by so many who call themselves Agnostics to explain to the religious world that they are not atheists, is almost enough to prove this. Indeed, the position is well summed up by Mr. John M. Robertson:—

The best argument for the use of the name Agnostic is simply that the word Atheist has been so long covered with all manner

147

of ignorant calumny that it is expedient to use a new term which though in some respects faulty, has a fair start, and will in time have a recognized meaning. The case, so stated, is reasonable; but there is the *per contra* that whatever the motive with which the name is used, it is now tacked to half a dozen conflicting forms of doctrine, varying loosely between Theism and Pantheism. The name of Atheist escapes that drawback. Its unpopularity has saved it from half-hearted and half-minded patronage.

So that, on the best showing, we are to take "Agnostic" on the professed ground that it is more exact than "Atheism," but on the real ground that it is less unpopular, waiting meanwhile for the time when it shall have become more exact than it is by becoming accepted in the same sense as the Atheism that has previously been rejected. Courage and straightforwardness saves a lot of trouble.

Mr. Bailey Saunders (*Quest of Faith*, p. 7) calls agnosticism "a plea on behalf of suspended judgment," and this is a favourite expression. It gives one an air of impartiality, with the comforting reflection that it will please the socially stronger side. But suspended judgment on what? To hold one's judgment in suspense implies that we have at least a workable comprehension of the subject in dispute, and that judgment is suspended because the evidence produced is not adequate to command decision. But is that the case here? Does the Agnostic claim that the evidence produced by the theist is merely inadequate, or that it is irrelevant? Surely he holds the latter position. And if that is the case, then he does not suspend judgment, for the simple reason that there is no case made out concerning which judgment is to be suspended. There is simply no case before the court. For the Agnostic, no more than the Atheist, can attach no intelligible meaning to "God." He must have it defined to understand it, and when it is defined he rejects it without ceremony. And it is quite obvious that when an Agnostic says, "I know nothing about God," he means more than that; otherwise it would not be worth the saying. He really means that no one else knows either. He asserts that a knowledge of god is impossible to anyone, because it does not present the possibility of being known. "God," standing alone is a meaningless word, and how can one suspend judgment concerning the truth of an unintelligible proposition?

For here are the plain facts of the situation. If we ask the Agnostic whether he suspends judgment concerning the existence of the gods of any savage peoples, the reply is in the negative. If we put the same question concerning the god of the Bible, or of the Mohammedan, or of any other of the world's theologies we receive the same answer. There is nothing here to suspend judgment about, the characters and qualities of the gods being such that there admits of no doubt as to their imaginary character. Or if it is said that the Agnostic, while dismissing the gods of the various theologies, savage and civilized, as being impossible, suspends judgment as to the existence of a "supreme mind," or of a "creative intelligence," the reply is that one cannot suspend judgment as to the possible existence of an inconceivability. For "mind" must be mind, as we know it. And it is a downright absurdity to speak of the possible existence of a "mind" while divesting it of all the qualities that characterize mind as we know it. Really between the statement that A. does not exist, and the affirmation that A. does exist, but differs in every conceivable particular from all known A.'s there is no difference whatever. We are denying its existence in the very act of affirming it.

Further, we quite agree with Mr. F. C. S. Schiller (*Riddles of the Sphinx*, pp. 17-19) that in practice such suspense of judgment is impossible. We suspend our judgment as to whether we shall die to-morrow or at some indefinite future date, and for that reason we make our arrangements in view of either contingency. We suspend judgment as to the honesty of an employee, and our attitude towards him is governed by that fact. And so with the question of a god. In one way or another we are bound to indicate our judgment on the subject. We must act either as though we believe in the possibility or in the impossibility of "divine" interference. If the mental hesitancy of the respectable Agnostic were accompanied by a corresponding timidity in action life would be impossible.

A less common plea on behalf of Agnosticism, but one on which a word must be said, is that the agnostic attitude is more "reverential" than that of atheism. But why in the name of all that is reasonable should one profess reverence towards something of which one knows nothing? Reverence, to be intelligible, must be directed towards an intelligent object, and we must have grounds for believing it to be worthy of reverence. Reverence towards our fellow creatures is a reasonable enough sentiment, but what is there reasonable in an expression of reverence towards something that can only be thought of—and even this is unwarranted—as a force? The truth is that this expression of reverence is no more than the flickering survival of religion. Numbers have reached the stage at which they can perceive the unreasonable nature of religious beliefs, but they have not yet managed to achieve liberation from the traditional emotional attitude towards these beliefs. In other words, the development of the emotional and the intellectual sides of their nature have been unequal, and for these the "Unknowable" has simply served as a peg on which to hang religious feelings that have been robbed of all intellectual support. The semi-religious Agnostic thus represents a transition form, interesting enough to all who observe how curiously decaying types strive to perpetuate themselves, but which is bound to disappear in the process of intellectual evolution.

Finally, one would like from the Agnostic some authoritative announcement as to his position in relation to what is known concerning the origin of the god-idea. So far as professed theists are concerned one expects this to be ignored. On the part of non-theists one expects a more logical attitude. In this case it is common ground with the Atheist and the Agnostic that the idea of god owes its beginnings to the ignorance of primitive man. We know the facts on which this idea was based, and we know that all these are now differently explained. The belief that there is a god governing nature is just one of those blunders made by primitive man, and is on all fours with the numerous other blunders he makes concerning himself and the world around him. Knowing this, and accepting this, believing that "god" springs from the same set of conditions that gave rise to fairies and spirits of various kinds, one would like to know on what ground the Agnostic definitely rejects the grounds on which the idea of god is based, while professing a state of suspended judgment about the existence of the object created by this primitive blunder. It is certainly surprising to find those who accept the natural origin of the god-idea, when they come to deal with current religion talk as though it were merely a question of the inconclusiveness of religious arguments. It is nothing of the kind. The final reply to the arguments set forth on behalf of Theism is, not that they are inconclusive, but that they are absolutely irrelevant to the question at issue. We cannot remain undecided because there is nothing to remain undecided about. We know that the idea of god is pure myth, and was never anything but myth. A belief that began in error, and which has no other basis than error, cannot by any possible argument be converted into a truth. The old question was, "Can man by searching find out God?" The modern answer is an emphatic affirmative. Substantially we have by searching found out God. We know the origin and history of one of the greatest delusions that ever possessed the human mind. God has been found out. Analytically and synthetically we understand the god-idea as previous generations could not understand it. It has been explained; and the logical consequence of the explanation is— Atheism.

Ultimately, then, we come to this: (1) The Agnosticism that concerns itself with a confession of ignorance concerning the nature of "existence," has no necessary connection with religion, and is only made to have such by a confusion of two distinct things. (2) The plea of a suspended judgment is invalid, since there is nothing about which one can suspend a decision. (3) The Agnosticism that professes a semi-religious feeling of reverence towards the "Unknowable" is fundamentally upon all fours with the religious feelings of the ordinary believer. Worshipping the Unknowable is more ridiculous than worshipping Huxley's "wilderness of apes." The apes *might* take some intelligent interest in the antics of their devotees; but to print our hypostatized ignorance in capital letters and then profess a feeling of veneration for it is as ridiculous a proceeding as the world has seen. After all, an absurdity is never quite so grotesque as when it is tricked out in scientific phrases and paraded as the outcome of profound philosophic thinking. (4) The only Agnosticism that seems capable of justifying itself is an Agnosticism that is indistinguishable from Atheism. To again cite Professor Flint, Atheist "means one who does not believe in God, and it means neither more nor less." The Agnostic is also one who is without belief in a god, every argument he uses to justify his position is and has been used as a justification of Atheism. Atheist is really "a thoroughly honest, unambiguous term," it admits of no paltering and of no evasion, and the need of the world, now as ever, is for clear-cut issues and unambiguous speech.

Chapter XIV

Atheism and Morals

Looking at the world as it is one cannot forbear a mild wonder at the fears expressed at the probable consequences to morals of a general acceptance of Atheism. One would have thought that the world would not run a very great danger of becoming worse on that account, and that, seeing the way in which all forms of rascality have flourished, and still maintain themselves, without in the least disturbing people's religious convictions, one might even feel inclined to risk a change in the hopes of improvement. Mainly, indeed, one might say that those who are affected by religious belief are such as can very well do without it, while those who stand in urgent need of moral improvement seldom show that their religious belief has any very beneficial effect on their conduct.

Yet nothing is more common than to find the theist, when driven off all other grounds of defense, protesting against a deliberate propaganda of Atheism on the ground of its probable harmful consequences to morals. This, not because those who have publicly professed Atheism are open to the charge of loose living, but on account of those who at present believe in religion, and whose loss of belief would possibly upset their moral equilibrium. It is a curious position for a theist to take up, since it implies that while the Atheist as we know him shows no deterioration of character in consequence of his loss of belief, we cannot be so certain of the present believers in deity. They are formed of poorer clay, and once convinced that there is no God with whom they have to reckon, there is no telling what will happen. So we are urged to let well alone, and leave believers with their illusions lest their loss should present us with a very unpleasant reality.

This fear is expressed in various ways, but in one way or another it is tolerably common. The following which reached me from a well known man of letters probably puts the argument as fairly and as temperately as it can be put, and therefore in dealing with that I cannot be accused of taking the theist at an unfair advantage. His conclusions are summarized in the following paragraphs. (The summary is the author's, not mine.)

(1) The decent-ish code of morals which prevails in this twentieth century is the outcome of all the human ages. From the very first, everywhere and all the time, it has, and continues to be, inextricably intertwined and influenced by Theistic beliefs, even when and where such beliefs have been the crudest and most debased form of polytheism.

(2) The ethical atmosphere in which we now live, after having had such an origin and history, remains strongly and frankly pervaded by religion of a Theistic type. Atheist, Agnostic, and Theist alike have to live in this atmosphere, and consciously or unconsciously, are subject to its influence.

(3) Even if we could set up a wholly secular code of morals, derived entirely from the exigencies of, tribal, communal, and national life, I take it that such a code would be inadequate to form the type of individual character we most admire, and

which acts under a sense of "ought" rather than of "must." The latter is often the mere demand of gregarious or individual comfort and convenience; the former may be quite opposed to the inclinations of the individual, and yet bring into play irksome but ennobling springs of action which a purely secular code cannot touch.

Now these statements put the case for the theist as moderately and as well as it can be put, and I think that they are worthy of a little careful examination. It may be observed that there is no insinuation that Atheists are actually worse than other people, only the fear that in the absence of some form of theism the higher ethical motive cannot be roused, and that therefore character will suffer. Well, we are none of us free from the contagion of our environment, and the most powerful influences are often enough those that it would be difficult to specify in any given instance. It is not only that the influence of the higher members of society affect the lower. The lower is not without its influence on the higher. But the question here is not really whether we are all exposed to the general influence of the group to which we belong, that, I think, is undeniable, the real question at issue is whether the determining influence on conduct is theistic or not. And I think it will be found that while the one thing is asserted it is the other that is proven.

So far as the first proposition is concerned it may be taken for granted that our present state is the product of all past evolution, and that in the course of that evolution theistic beliefs have been closely—not inextricably—connected with morals. But this is not alone true of morality, it is true of every branch of human thought and of every aspect of human life. Art, science, literature, have all been closely connected with religious beliefs. Necessarily so. Early human history is spent under the shadow of superstition, and its dominating influence affects the form of every aspect of life. But as the course of development has been to separate the essential from the non-essential and to place most of each department of life on a self-supporting basis, it would not seem an unreasonable conclusion that ethics will follow the same lines. In fact, it is following the same lines. There are few educated people nowadays who would claim that morality cannot exist apart from religion, they are content to say, as my correspondent does, that in the absence of religion belief the higher aspects of morality will suffer.

Our morality, we are told, is the outcome of all the human ages. I go further than that and assert that it is the outcome of all the human and of all the animal ages. There is no break in nature, and to the evolutionist the development of the human from the animal is plain. And it should scarcely need pointing out nowadays that nearly every one of the fundamental qualities of man can be seen in germ in the animal world. I only emphasize the point here because it is so often forgotten that morality is fundamentally the expression of those conditions under which associated life is found possible and profitable, and that so far as any quality is declared to be moral its justification and meaning must be found in that direction. The question of incentive we will come to later; for the moment it is enough to insist upon the fact that morality is fashioned, in its fundamentals, with reference to facts, not with reference to speculative beliefs. Beliefs may influence morality for awhile, but the persistent operation of social selection secures a general conformity between conduct and the conditions upon which life depends. That is the fundamental fact to be remembered in all discussions of morality, although it is the fact that is most often ignored. Ultimately life determines moral teaching, it is not moral teaching that determines life.

Life not alone determines morality, but it determines religion as well. What else is the meaning of all those discarded forms

156

of religious belief, those bodies of dead gods, that meet the student of history as the remains of extinct animals meet the geologist in his unravelment of the story of the earth's vicissitudes? They are the result of a lack of adaptation to new conditions to which they could not accommodate themselves. Once the gods lorded it over man as the gigantic dinosaur lorded it in his day over lesser animals. And in the one case, as in the other, a change in the environment brought about their doom. Natural selection determines the survival of religions as of animal forms, and a religion to survive must become increasingly utilitarian in character, certainly there is a point beyond which the opposite tendency cannot be carried.

Assume, for example, that a religion existed of a grossly anti-social character, one that teaches doctrines that are subversive of the general social well-being. One of two things must result. If the religion is strong enough to enforce its teaching the society it dominates will disappear, and the religion will die out with it. If, on the other hand, it cannot enforce its teaching, or can get it accepted only in a modified form, then either the religion disappears in its original form, or it is modified to get itself established. To live, religion must establish some sort of harmony between its teachings and the conditions of life. It may retard the development of life, but it must not retard to the point of destruction. This is all that is really involved in what is called the purification of religious teaching. In reality there is no such thing. The purification is a modification, and it is modified in order that it may become acceptable to the society in which it is existing. The ascetic epidemic, the various disgusting sects that have sprung into existence from time to time during the course of Christian history, have all died out from this cause. As with the individual, so with society, the forces of which we are conscious generally move upon the surface. Of the underlying ones we are mostly unaware.

157

The truth is, then, that behind all our consciously elaborated theories of life there are operative the unconscious or subconscious forces of evolution. There is, of course, a certain area of conduct in which speculative opinions play their part, and where actions may be arbitrarily classed as good or bad. But this area is, of necessity, limited, and for the reasons that have been given above. Properly understood morality is not something very abstract, but something that is very concrete. The underlying reason for morality is always the same, and we are compelled to hark back to it for justification. And no rejection of religion can alter the basis upon which morality rests.

The proposition that Atheist, Agnostic, and Theist breathe the same atmosphere and are affected by the same influences is, therefore, one that is two-edged. If our intellectual atmosphere is saturated with religious influences, it is also saturated with social influences of a much more fundamental character, and which have been perpetually correcting religious extravagances. And it is at least open to the Atheist to retort that we have to thank this circumstance that religious beliefs have not been more injurious than has been actually the case. If, for example, the ascetic epidemic of the early Christian centuries had increased in force and had continued operative, European society would have disappeared. That this was not the case was due to the strength of the sexual and social instincts, against which religion was unable to maintain its hold. In the change of opinion over the better way to spend Sunday, or in the decay of the doctrine of eternal damnation, we have the same point illustrated. Right through history it has been the social instincts that have acted as a corrective to religious extravagance. And it is worth noting that with the exception of a little gain from the practice of casuistry, religions have contributed nothing towards the building up of a science of ethics. On the contrary it has been a very potent cause of

158

confusion and obstruction. Fictitious vices and virtues have been created and the real moral problem lost sight of. It gave the world the morality of the prison cell, instead of the tonic of the rational life. And it was indeed fortunate for the human race that conduct was not ultimately dependent upon a mass of teachings that had their origin in the brains of savages, and were brought to maturity during the darkest period of European civilization.

In dealing with the two first propositions I have, by implication, answered the third—namely, that a wholly secular authentic code of morals would be inadequate to form the highest type of character; it might supply a "must," but it could not supply an "ought."

The first and obvious reply to an objection of this kind is that our working code of morals is secular already. In life, if we observe without prejudice, it is not difficult to see that one's neighbors, friends, social class, etc., have far more force in shaping conduct than speculative theories. In its widest sense natural selection determines what actions shall be declared to be moral. Of this we may take the universal feeling against homicide. This is but an expression of the truth that social life would be impossible were it otherwise. And when we pass from the general to the special we meet with much the same principle operating in society. The average burglar pursues his calling with no special sense of its wrongness, although he may have a keen sense of its dangers. But while burgling with a fairly easy conscience, he does flinch at breaking the code of honor set up by his fellow-burglars. And at the other extreme we have the "gentleman" with his code of honor which forbids him not to pay a gambling debt, but takes no count of keeping a poor tradesman out of his money. In each of these cases the determining factor is not theory but fact, and the fact here is association with our fellow countrymen or with a special social class. Morality, in short, is social or nothing. Moral laws are meaningless apart from social life. Every moral command implies the existence of a social medium, and it is no more than a study in history to see how this social medium has been continuously shaping and reshaping human nature. The determination here is not conscious, but it is real, however much disguised it may be by various forms or theories. And when we realize this, it is no more than a truism to say that a change in religious belief can no more destroy morality than a change in government can destroy society.

But in saying that the essence of morality is unreasoning I do not mean that it is unreasonable. All I mean is that it can receive a reasonable justification, and that no matter how lofty the development it has its basis in the fundamental conditions of associated animal and human life. We may surround the subject with a vague and attractive idealistic verbalism, but we come back to this as a starting point. The love of family, with all its attendant values, rests upon the fact of crude sexual desire, refined, of course, during the passing of many generations, but dependent upon it all the same. Remove the sexual desire and the family feelings are inexplicable. Thus, the *reason* for the existence of the sexual instinct is race preservation, but the end has been achieved in a quite unreasoning manner. In the animal world at large there is certainly no conscious desire for the production of offspring, nor is there with the mass of human beings. There is the desire to gratify an impulse, and very little more. And for the strengthening of an instinct there need not be, nor is there, any consciousness of its social value. All that is necessary is that it shall be useful. Natural selection attends to the rest.

This will, I think, supply an answer to the contention that secular ethics can supply a "must," but not an "ought"; that is, it may show that an individual should act in accordance with his inclinations, but in cases where these clash with the social well being, it can supply no reason why the former should give way to the latter.

The argument rests upon a dual confusion. First, the moral "ought" is no more than an organized and conscious form of "must," and not something distinct from it. One may test the matter by taking a case. A man says, I ought so to work as to promote the general welfare of society. If we seek to find the source of this feeling we come ultimately upon the feeling of tribal solidarity in virtue of which certain tribes survive in the struggle for existence. It is gregariousness struggling into consciousness. The moral "ought" is an idealized form of the primitive tribal "must." And the "must" of primitive life is encouraged and developed because it is one of the conditions of survival.

The second point of confusion is based upon a supposed opposition between individual inclinations and an ideal conception of duty. That the two are often, as a matter of fact, in conflict, must be admitted. And the cause is that while our inclinations represent a heritage from the past, our ideals are a projection into the future. But the contention is based upon their supposed permanent hostility, and that need not be taken for granted. For the whole course of social evolution tends to bring about a substantial identification of personal and social well-being. More and more as the human race develops it is being recognized that there is no real individual life apart from social life, of which it is the creation and the expression. Such antagonism as exists is the inevitable result of a conflict between an organism and its adaptation to a changing environment. And from this point of view the whole growth of man is in the nature of an expansion of his sympathies and sense of duty over an ever-widening area. The primitive egoism of the tribal individual is extended to the nation, that of the nation to the empire, and thence to the whole of humanity. There is no destruction or denial of self in such cases, it is a development of the sense of self over an enlarging area.

Finally, if a secular code of morals will not suffice, it is sheer rhetoric to say that religion is powerful enough to operate where naturalism fails. On the contrary, in a civilized community religious appeals tend to become secular appeals in disguise. On the admission of Christian advocates the two most powerful appeals that can be made are on the one hand, in the name of the fatherhood of god, and on the other, the conception of the Mother and the Child. And what are these but appeals to the secular and social feelings of man in the name of religion? It may be granted that Atheism in its appeals to mankind often fails, but in this respect is it any worse off than religion? Why, one of the standing complaints of religious preachers in all ages is that their message falls so frequently on deaf ears. There is no more certainty that the religious appeal will meet with success, than there is that any other appeal will be successful. And there is the unquestionable fact that morality has become stronger as the power of religion has weakened. The higher qualities have asserted themselves during a period of religious disintegration, and the student of morals sees in this a promise of a further development in the future.

And to all prophecies as to the effects of Atheism on the morality of the future there is the apt reply that they are prophecies and nothing else. And in this respect it is dangerous for the Christian theist to appeal to history. For while the consequences of Atheism can be no more than a forecast, which may or may not be justified, the record of Christianity is before the world. And we know that the period during which the influence of Christian theism was strongest, was the period when the intellectual life of civilized man was at its lowest, morality at its weakest, and the general outlook most hopeless. Religious control gave us heresy hunts, and Jew hunts, burnings for witchcraft, and magic in the place of medicine. It gave us the Inquisition and the *auto da fé*, the fires of Smithfield and the night of St. Bartholomew. It gave us the war of sects and it helped powerfully to establish the sect of war. It gave us life without happiness, and death cloaked with terror. The Christian record is before us, and it is such that every Church blames the others for its existence. Quite as certainly we cannot point to a society that has been dominated by Freethinking ideas, but we can point to their existence in all ages, and can show that all progress is due to their presence. We can show that progressive ideas have originated with the least, and have been opposed by the most religious sections of society. What religion has done for the world we know; what free thought will do we can only guess. But we are confident that as honesty is possible without the falsity of religion, as duty may be done with no other incentive than its visible consequences on the people around us, so life may be lived in honor and closed in peace with no other inspiration than comes from the contemplation of the human stream from which we emerge and into which we finally go.

Chapter XV

Atheism Inevitable

Between Theism and Atheism the logical mind may halt, but it cannot rest for long, and in the end the logic of fact works its way. Compromise, while it may delay the end without preventing its inevitability, is quite out of place in matters of the intellect. In the world of practice compromise is often unavoidable, but in that of ideas the sole concern should be for truth. When Whately said that the man who commenced by loving Christianity more than truth would continue by loving his own sect more than any other, and end by loving himself more than all, he placed his finger on the great moral danger of compromise where opinion is concerned. It begins, ostensibly, by considering the respect due to an opponent's case, it continues by sacrificing the respect that is due one's own, and it ends by giving a new sense of value to the very opinion it aims at destroying. "No quarter" is the only sound rule in intellectual warfare, where to take prisoners is only one degree less dishonoring than to be taken captive oneself. And the value of an opinion is never wholly in the opinion itself. No small part of its worth is derived from the way in which it is held, and the importance which is placed upon it.

When Professor Tylor said that the deepest of all divisions in the history of human thought was that which divided Animism from Materialism, he was saying what I have been endeavoring to say, in another manner, in the foregoing pages. Atheism and supernaturalism are fundamental divisions in human thought, and divisions that connote an irreconcilable antagonism. The terms not only mark a division, they are the badges of a movement, the indication of a pilgrimage. Dr. Tylor's own work and the work of his fellow laborers tell the story in detail, and although no one is in a position to write "finis" to it, there is no doubt as to what its end will be. And the manner of the pilgrimage is quite plain. The starting point is the creation by the befogged ignorance of primitive man of that welter of ghosts and gods which make so much of early existence a veritable nightmare. The journey commences in a world in which the "supernatural" is omnipresent, in which man's chief endeavors is given to win the good will or avert the anger of the ghosts and gods to whom he has himself given being. And the end, the last stage of the pilgrimage, is a world in which mechanical operations take the place of disembodied intelligences, or of supernatural powers. From a world in which the gods are everything and do everything to a world in which the gods are nothing and do nothing. The story of that transition is the record of one of the greatest revolutions that has happened in the history of mankind. Its real greatness and far-reaching significance is not always adequately recognized, even by those who welcome it gladly. Indeed, the narrower interests that suffer from this revolution are more keenly alive to its importance than are those who benefit from its consummation. That is, perhaps, what one ought to expect from the known course of human history. For history would not be what it is, nor would reforms be so difficult of accomplishment were it not possible to persuade the slave that his servitude guards him from the very evils it perpetuates.

Incidentally the nature of that revolution has been indicated in the preceding pages. But a more connected view will form a fitting close to this work. Nothing more than the barest of outlines can be attempted, but such as it is it may serve to illustrate the truth that Atheism is more than the speculative philosophy of a few, that it is in sober truth the logical outcome of mental growth. So far as any phase of human life can be called inevitable Atheism may lay claim to being inescapable. All mental growth can be seen leading to it, just as we can see one stage of social development giving a logical starting point for another stage, and which could have been foretold had our knowledge of all the forces in operation been precise enough. Atheism is, so to speak, implicit in the growth of knowledge; its complete expression is the consummation of a process that began with the first questionings of religion. And the completion of the process means the death of supernaturalism in all its forms.

Religion, it has already been said, is something that is acquired, and although that sounds little better than a commonplace, yet reflection proves it to contain an important truth. For it is in the nature of the acquisition that its significance lies. Whatever be the earliest stages of religion it is at all events clear that its earliest form is in the nature of a hypothesis, even though only of the semi-conscious kind that exists when man is brought into touch with some new and overpowering experience. Religious ideas are put forth in explanation of something. But all explanation whether by savage or civilized man, must be in terms of existing knowledge. No other method is possible. We must explain the unknown in terms of the known, and our explanation will be the more elaborate and the nearer the truth as our knowledge of the nature of the forces are the more exact and extensive. A knowledge of the laws of condensation and evaporation enables a modern to give an explanation of the meaning of a shower of rain that is simply impossible to man in an earlier stage of culture. In every case the facts are the

166

same, and in each case the explanation given depends upon the knowledge acquired.

Now one radical distinction between an early and a modern explanation of the world is that whereas the former moves from within outward, the latter moves from without inward. Uncivilized man explains the world by himself; civilized man explains himself by the world. The savage describes the world in terms of his own feelings and passions, the scientist regards human qualities as resulting from the relation which man holds to the forces around him. The process, while presenting a radical difference in form, is yet fundamentally one in essence. Ignorant of all that we connote by such an expression as "natural forces," whatever explanation is offered by the savage is necessarily in terms of the only force with which he is acquainted. But it happens that the only forces which he then fancies he understands are those represented by his own organization. What he is conscious of doing is prompted by his own will and intelligence. He hurts when he is angry, he rewards when he is pleased, and he makes the same assumption regarding the things around him. So far as he explains nature he vitalizes it. Vital force becomes the symbol of all force. And this result expresses a mental law that is universally operative. The civilized mind differs from the savage mind not because the brain functions differently in the two cases, but solely in consequence of the wider and truer knowledge of the causes of natural phenomena which civilized man possesses. We arrive at different conclusions because we start from different premises. Inevitably, therefore, the first attempt of man to deal with nature takes the form of assuming the operation of a number of personal intelligences. Natural objects are alive, and everything that happens to man, from the cradle to the grave, is thought of as being either alive or controlled by living beings. The world is filled with a crowd of ghostly beings exercising more or less discordant functions.

Against this riot of gods the conception of natural law develops but slowly. Quite apart from the natural inertia of the human mind, the fact of questioning the power of these assumed beings involves to the primitive mind an element of grave danger. All sorts of things may happen if the gods are offended, and in self-defense the tribe feels bound to suppress the critic of religion and of religious ideas. But once the step is taken, the area over which the gods rule is to that extent restricted, and with that step Atheism may be said to be born.

What Lange said in the opening sentences of his classic "History of Materialism," that "Materialism is as old as philosophy, but not older," may be said with equal truth of Atheism. That, too, is as old as philosophy, since it begins with man's attempts to break away from that primitive interpretation of nature which sees in all phenomena the action of personal intelligences. It is of no importance in which branch of knowledge the departure was made, whichever department one takes the process can be seen at work. Astronomy appears to have been the branch of knowledge in which the powers of the gods were earliest restricted, although it was not until the discoveries of Copernicus, Galileo, Newton, and Laplace were given to the world that "God" vanished altogether from that region. Geology follows with the teaching that chemical, thermal, and other known forces leave nothing for the gods to accomplish. Biology and sociology, dealing with more complex forces, are much later in the field, but they tread the same path. They provide a refuge for "God" for awhile, but it is evident that their complete dispossession is no more than a question of time. And even though the very complex character of the forces working in these latter departments should prevent us ever acquiring the same degree of prevision that exists in other classes, no difference will be made to the general result. The principle will be fairly established and our ignorance of details will no longer be made the ground for assertions which, if made at all, should rest upon the most exact knowledge. "God" will be left with nothing to do, and man will not for ever go on worshipping a God whose sole recommendation is that he exists, nor will the common sense of civilized people hold on to a hypothesis when there is nothing left for that hypothesis to explain.

The single and outstanding characteristic of the conception of god at all times and under all conditions is that it is the equivalent of ignorance. In primitive times it is ignorance of the character of natural forces that leads to the assumption of the existence of gods, and in this respect the god-idea has remained true to itself throughout. Even to-day whenever the principle of "God" is invoked a very slight examination is enough to show that the only reason for this being done is our ignorance of the subject before us. Why does anyone assume that we must believe in God in order to explain the beginnings of life? Why is "God" assumed to be responsible for the order of nature? Why must we assume "God" to explain mind? The answer to these and to all similar questions is that we do not know, in the sense that we know the cause of planetary motions, how these things came to be. It is not what we know about them that leads to the assumption of god, but what we do not know. And the converse of that is that so soon as knowledge replaces ignorance "God" will be dispensed with. It is never a case of believing in God because of the actual knowledge we possess, but always the appeal to weakness and ignorance. From this point of view the colloquial "God only knows!" expresses the appeal to ignorance even more clearly than the elaborate argument of the sophisticated apologist.

This aspect of the matter was well put by Spinoza. Believers in the argument from design, he says, have a method of argument that is a reduction, not to the impossible, but to ignorance. Thus,

If a stone falls from a roof on to someone's head and kills him, they will demonstrate by their new method that the stone fell to kill the man; for if it had not by God's will fallen with that object, how could so many circumstances (and there are often many concurrent circumstances) have all happened together by chance. Perhaps you will answer that the event is due to the facts that the wind was blowing, and the man was walking that way. "But why," they will insist, "was the wind blowing, and why was the wind at that very time blowing that way?" If you again answer, that the wind had then sprung up because the sea had begun to be agitated the day before, the weather having been previously calm, and that the man had been invited by a friend, they will again insist: "But why was the sea agitated, and why was the man invited at that time?" So they will pursue their question from cause to cause, till at last you take refuge in the will of God—in other words, the sanctuary of ignorance. (Appendix to *Ethics*; pt. 1)

The sanctuary of ignorance "God" has always been, and the sanctuary of ignorance it will remain to the end. It has no other function in life. A consciousness of this is shown by the upholders of Theism in the eagerness with which they welcome every supposed demonstration of the impotence of science, and of the resistance everywhere offered to the development of scientific advance.

So far, then, as the progress of life makes for the growth of knowledge, so far may we safely claim that the development of thought makes for Atheism, as we have just said, and to do the religious world justice it has always been quick to realize this, and every great scientific generalization—as well as many smaller ones, has been resisted on the ground that they were atheistic in character and tended to take the control of the world out of God's hands. Present-day theists are apt to condemn this attitude of their predecessors, but it can hardly be denied that the logic lies with the earlier representatives. A God who does nothing might, for all practical purposes, as well be non-existent. And a God who is merely in the background of things, who may be responsible for their origin, but having originated them surrenders all control over their operations, is hardly more serviceable. The modern theist saves his God only by leaving him a negligible quantity in a universe he is supposed to sustain and govern.

And it cannot be too often emphasized that the whole basis of exact or positive science is atheistic—that is, it is compelled to ignore even the possibility of the existence of God. Every scientific generalization rests upon the constancy of natural forces. On no other basis is it possible to give a scientific interpretation to what has gone before or to anticipate what is to happen in the future. Every scientific calculation assumes that in the world with which it deals causation is invariable and universal. But if we are to assume the operations of a "God" at any time or point every scientific calculation would have to be accompanied with the D.V. of a prayer meeting. To argue from the past to the future would be futile. God might have operated then, no one could be certain he will operate now. Or he might have operated in the far past, but he might not in the future. In either case the assumption of a God would be fatal to exact scientific calculations. Thus in sheer self defense, in order to preserve its character as science, science is compelled to discard even the possibility of the existence of a controlling intelligence. As one eminent theistic advocate admits, "Science has no need, and indeed, can make no use, in any particular instance of the theistic hypothesis."[6] It is only when supernaturalism is partly excluded from human thought that science can be said to really commence its existence; and in proportion as our conception of the universe becomes that of

---

[6] Prof. Ward "Naturalism and Agnosticism" Vol. I., p. 23.

an aggregate of non-conscious forces—or of a single force with many forms producing given results under given conditions, only then does our view of the universe reach completion.

A study of the nature and tendency of human development does, therefore, provide a very strong presumption in favor of atheism. All growth here is in favor of atheism and away from theism. In the beginning we have the gods everywhere and dominating everything. They do everything and control everything. "God" is the one universal primitive hypothesis. And all subsequent development is to its discrediting. There is no growth in the idea of god, there is only an attenuation. The gods grow fewer as the human race approaches maturity. Their activities cease as man becomes aware of the character of the forces around him. And it may be further noted that this decline of the belief in deity is brought about as much by sheer pressure of experience as by pure reason. The majority of people do not reason themselves out of the belief in god, they outgrow it. People cease to believe in the gods because they experience no compulsion to believe in them. The logic of fact is ultimately more powerful than the logic of theory, and as environmental forces brought the gods into existence, so environmental forces carry them out again.

Now Atheism does but make explicit in words what has long been implicit in practice. It takes the god-idea, examines it, and explains it out of existence. It admits the reality of gods as it admits the reality of ghosts and fairies and witches. They are subjective, not objective, realities. Atheism takes the god-idea, explains its origin, describes its subsequent development, and in so doing indicates its ultimate fate. In this sense Atheism is, as I have said, no more than the final stage of a long historical process. The theistic phase of thought is an inevitable one in human evolution, but it is no more a permanent one than is the belief in hobgoblins. One might here paraphrase Bacon and say, "A little philosophy inclineth a man to belief in the gods, but depth in philosophy leads to their rejection as a false and useless hypothesis." It is true that thinking brought the gods into the world; it is also true that adequate thinking carries them out again.

The cardinal truth is, of course, that the hypothesis of mind in nature does not owe its existence to an exact knowledge of things but to its absence. Its origin must be sought in a pre-scientific age and its persistence in a number of extraneous circumstances which have perpetuated a belief that would otherwise have inevitably disappeared. And it would indeed be a matter for surprise if this belief—said by theists to be of all beliefs the most profound—should be the one speculation on which savage thought has justified itself. On no other question did the primitive mind reach truth. Universally its speculations concerning the world were discovered to be wrong. On this one topic we are asked to believe that the savage was absolutely right.

From the age of fetichism—rightly called by Comte the creative age in theology—the history of the god-idea has been a history of a series of modifications and rejections. Scarce an invention that has not slain a god, scarce a discovery has not marked the burying-place of a discarded deity. Criticism reduced the gods in number and limited them in power. Advancing knowledge pushed them back till nature, "rid of her haughty lords," is conceived as a huge mechanism, self-acting, self-adjusting, and self-repairing. Even in the mouths of religionists "God" to-day stands for little more than a force. We must not describe him as personal, as intelligent, or as conscious, and between this and the existence assumed by atheistic science it is impossible to detect any vital difference. Atheism, then, takes its stand upon the observed trend of human history, upon a scrutiny of the facts of nature, and upon an examination of the origin and contents of the god-idea. And upon these grounds it may fairly claim to be irrefutable and inevitable. Circumstances may obstruct its universal acceptance as a reasoned mental attitude, but that merely delays, it does not destroy the certainty of its final triumph.

With the supposed direful consequences that would follow the triumph of Atheism I have not dealt with at length. These are the bugbears which the designing normally employ in order to frighten the timid and credulous. Mental uprightness and moral integrity are certainly not the property of one religion, nor can it be said with truth that they belong to any. And examining the histories of religion it is a fair assumption that in whatever direction the world may suffer from the disappearance of religion there will be no moral catastrophe. Looking at the whole course of human history, and noting how the vilest and most ruinous practices have been ever associated with religion, and have ever relied upon religion for support, the cause for speculation is, not what will happen to the world when religion dies out, but how human society has managed to flourish while the belief in the gods ruled.

Fortunately for human society nature has not left the operation of the fundamental virtues dependent upon the acceptance of this or that theory of the world. The social and family instincts, which are inseparable from our nature as men and women, and which operate in ways of which we are largely unconscious, are the grounds of all the higher and finer virtues, and while a change in opinion may affect their operation here and there, it can never alter their fundamental character. Conduct, in short, comes from life, it is not the creation of a theory to be dismissed by resolution or refashioned by a vote.

What Atheism would mean in practice would be an enormous concentration of energy upon purely human affairs, and a judgment of conduct in terms of human happiness and prosperity. And that certainly furnishes no cause for alarm. It is, indeed, our greatest need. We need an awakening to the untapped power and possibilities of human nature. If the gods die, man their creator still lives; and the creative energy which once covered the face of nature with innumerable gods, which spent itself in the attempt to win their favor, and which called forth a heaven in the endeavor to redress the wrongs of earth, may, if properly applied, yet cover the earth with homes in which men and women, rendered purer by love and stronger by knowledge, will rise superior to the fabled gods before whom they once bowed in blind adoration.